WILLIE MAYS:

COAST TO COAST GIANT

Known variously as "24" (his uniform number) and
"Wondrous Willie," Willie Mays was a big league star
beginning with his rookie year as a New York Giant. It
was a prompt success which won him another nickname,
"Instant Ballplayer." His consistently high batting average and his famous "basket catch" have made Willie Mays
prominent in a profession liberally studded with stars.
This up-to-date portrait of Willie Mays is written by a
devoted Giant fan and a man said by many to have written
more about the Giants than any other writer.

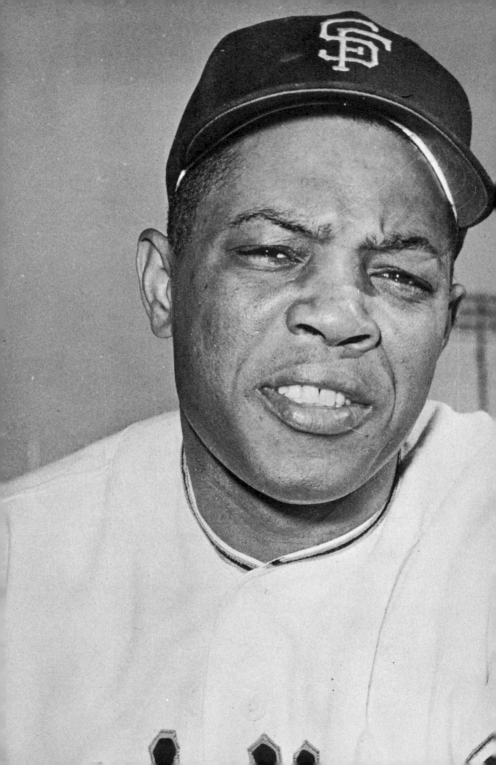

WILLIE MAYS:

COAST TO COAST GIANT

By Charles Einstein

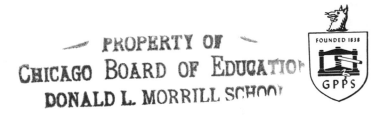
G. P. Putnam's Sons   New York

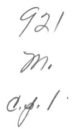

Ninth Impression

Published simultaneously in the Dominion of Canada
by Longmans Canada Limited, Toronto
Library of Congress Catalog Card Number: 63-9693
Manufactured in the United States of America
10-up

CONTENTS

WILLIE MAYS:

COAST TO COAST GIANT

Overleaf photo by CHARLES DOHERTY,
San Francisco Examiner

MAN ON HIS WAY TO WORK

It was a Saturday in May of 1961—a beautiful Saturday in San Francisco, with only a few traces of cloud and no fog. From the third floor of a spacious walk-up apartment on Spruce Street—a quiet, middle-class neighborhood about halfway between the Bay on the east and the ocean to the west—a man started down the stairs to go to work. The clock said a little after 10 o'clock in the morning.

The man got behind the wheel of a white Cadillac, which was parked across the street, facing south. He drove half a block to the intersection of California and turned left, continuing a little over a mile on California to the intersection of Gough Street. Here he turned right. Gough is a one-way street and feeds, about half a mile farther on, into the Central Freeway, which in turn feeds into the James Lick Freeway.

Southbound on the Lick, the Cadillac turned off at Silver Avenue, and a succession of back streets led the driver to the entrance of the parking lot at Candlestick Park—the rear entrance, back of center field.

The man at the gate grinned and waved and said, "Hit one today, Willie?"

"Sure," Willie Mays said. "Hit two." He uttered a short, high peal of laughter. He was a man happy with the day, happy in his work.

He drove to the players' parking area, left the car in its assigned, numbered slot, and was met by a small army of boys as he got out. They kept pace with him as he walked briskly to the players' entrance. From a distance, it looked like a forest moving, a small human forest surrounding Willie Mays. The branches of the trees in this forest were the arms of the small boys. The foliage was the scorecards, magazines, pictures, and scraps of paper they held aloft, vying for Willie's autograph.

Mays worked his way from the crush at last, heading through a fenced walkway to the clubhouse door. Inside, as you come through this door, on the right, is a door to the visiting team's clubhouse; on the left, is the door to the Giants' clubhouse; straight ahead is a tunnel leading to right field. It is this tunnel the visiting team uses in going to and from the playing field. The Giants themselves have their own tunnel, leading from their clubhouse to their dugout on the first-base side. It is this tunnel, of course, that they use. Remember these facts, for they have something to do with what happened on the field this day.

Mays' locker is one of six at the forefront of the spacious

clubhouse. The other five belonged, at this time, to coaches Salty Parker, Whitey Lockman, Larry Jansen, Wes Westrum, and to the old pro Harvey Kuenn. Only Westrum and Kuenn were there when Willie came in.

"Ho-oh," Mays said, by way of greeting, and stopped at the stool in front of his locker, looking down at the pile of mail that had been left for him there.

"Regulars hit at eleven," Westrum said to him.

"*Eleven!*" Mays said, incredulous. "What for? Nobody told me that."

"Pregame ceremonies," Westrum said. "They're going to make Alvin an honorary sheriff."

"Honorary *who?*" Mays giggled. "Cap gonna love that."

Cap is Alvin Dark, the manager of the San Francisco Giants. He earned the nickname as team captain of the Giant club that, in New York, won the pennant in 1951 and 1954.

"Well," Mays said, "gotta get dressed."

"Gotta do the job," Harvey Kuenn said. He reached for a plug of chewing tobacco. "Don't forget it's Saturday."

"Man," Mays said to him, "what you care what day it is?"

"I didn't say I cared," Kuenn said. "Gotta do the job, that's all."

Mays looked at him. "You working?"

"No," Harvey said.

Kuenn's knee was still tender. He had injured it two weeks before at Milwaukee, playing third base.

Today's opponent, at San Francisco, was that same Milwaukee club. In those three games at Milwaukee, Warren Spahn had no-hitted the Giants in one; Mays had hit four home runs in another. Last night, here in San Francisco, Spahn had defeated the Giants again, this time 5 to 4.

The significance of all this, to a man like Mays at this moment, was not that these two clubs had had some unusually exciting games so far this year, but that, instead, there would be no clubhouse meeting before today's game. Manager Dark would sit down for a few moments with pitching coach Jansen, catcher Ed Bailey, and today's Giant pitcher, Juan Marichal, to go over the way he wanted Marichal to work the Milwaukee hitters, but even that would be over quickly. Marichal had already faced the Braves once this year—in the middle game of those three at Milwaukee—and had beaten them 7–3 on a well-scattered yield of eight hits.

Mays now removed his tan polo shirt and brown slacks and began to dress. This was the second game of the current Giant home stand, but already there was a streak of grime on the left leg of his uniform pants. With the Giants trailing 4–2 last night, he had opened the home half of the sixth with a single. Felipe Alou had followed with a double-play ball to the shortstop, and Mays had gone into second in a cloud of dirt, trying to break it up.

The shirt, though, was still spanking clean. On the front, in black lettering with orange piping, it said G I A N T S. Blocked in the same color motif, on the back, was, in utmost simplicity, the most famous double number in baseball history—*24*.

"OH, I JUST LOVE DAYS LIKE THIS!"

Outside, the Giants were taking batting practice. As always, the regulars went first, and in batting order, and they were serious about it, as all ballplayers are about hitting practice. But the second and third times around they began to clown a fraction. "One out of the cage!" Mays yelled in his high voice to Stretch McCovey, the big first baseman. That meant, third time around, that each hitter was entitled to one ball that, not being missed or fouled, got out of the batting cage. Longest hit won the contest.

McCovey, a dead right-field pull hitter, swung late on a fast ball and arched a looper that fell just fair along the left-field line.

"Hello, double!" he cried.

"That don't make," Mays snapped. "We playing long ball."

"Two-base hit's a long ball," McCovey caroled, "where I come from."

"Where you come from?"

"Alabama, same as you."

"Mobile," Mays said. "That's where you come from."

"That's still Alabama," McCovey said.

After a time, the Braves took over for their hitting practice. Then it was time for fielding practice. Mays made four throws from center field, two to third base, two to home plate, but then, unlike the other regulars, went and stood behind first base, waiting to play that position with the scrubs when it came their turn to get their infield workout.

At one point, someone had said to Dark, "Why do you let him do that—fool around in the infield? You can get him tired. You can get him hurt."

"I know," Dark said. "Except for one thing."

"What's that?"

"He's Willie."

Now, manager Dark was standing at home plate, being made an honorary sheriff; the Giants were playing catch outside their dugout, ready to take the field. The crowd of 29,150 was restless, wanting the game to begin. They were anxious to see what they would see.

And to not see what they would not see, for much that is baseball goes overlooked by the spectators. It is there to see, but they are looking at something else.

Next time you go to a game and a man gets an extra-base hit, take your eye off the ball. Watch the first baseman and the first-base umpire as the hitter rounds the bag. They're not watching the ball. They seem to be looking at the ground in front of them. Actually, of course, they're both watching first base to see if the hitter touches it on his way around. This is automatic. But the fan never sees it. Not that he misses much—it's certainly not the most thrilling sight in the world—but it is emblematic of things that go on constantly all over the field.

Jog out to center field now with Willie Mays for this game against Milwaukee. You're Willie Mays. You stand at attention, cap over heart, facing the flagpole, while the band plays "The Star-Spangled Banner." Then you turn to watch your pitcher finish the last of his warm-up throws.

And now the lead-off batter comes up for the Braves— Lee Maye, a left-handed hitter.

To the fans, if they look at you at all, all you've done is set yourself in position in center field to await the outcome of the pitch.

The truth is that mentally, and with physical results, you have already catalogued four separate things in your mind:

One—The situation: score, inning, baserunners if any (and the individual running characteristics and capabilities of each), number of outs.

Two—The hitter: his typical strength, distance, direction.

Three—The climate: wind if any (particularly so at Candlestick); humidity (batted balls react differently in thick and thin air); soil conditions (soft or hard? what will the ground ball do?).

Four—Your pitcher *and his pitch* (your second baseman or shortstop will signal the pitch to you—the curve, fast ball, and change all will react differently when hit).

You will do this, pitch in and pitch out, the whole game long. To do this, you must play center field not only in terms of yourself but also in terms of your right and left fielders (is one of them weak moving toward center? if so, you have to shade him a step).

Yet these still may not be considered separate considerations. Let's take points two and four above—your hitter may have a weakness for a set-up (not only the kind of pitch, but where it is aimed) so that your pitcher will deliberately throw a ball one place to make the next pitch a strike somewhere else. But if the wind is blowing in (point three) at that moment, and if the score is 8–0 in your favor in the ninth inning, the need for the set-up may not even exist. Maybe your pitcher's got to do nothing but throw strikes.

Is it twilight in Los Angeles? The false light in the first inning of games that start there at 8 P.M. in June is a known condition in itself. Have you guarded against it? Is it the fifth inning in San Francisco in July? If so, the sun will be just over the last rise in the stands, and your dark glasses, swiveled up underneath the bill of your cap, must be flicked down instantly—another gesture the fan seldom if ever notices—so you can have a continuous bead on the ball, rather than have it "go blind" on you when it reaches a certain height. Have you built up a lead and now put a fast defensive third baseman in to replace the slower, big-hitting man who played that spot at the start? If so, your shortstop can now stop shading his third baseman—and you can stop shading your shortstop!

This unparalleled, endless concentration on details few spectators ever even think of exists, of course, mainly in the major leagues, and then, to its ultimate quintessence, only in the hands of a skilled handful. Little wonder the fan fails to notice it—it may pay off as seldom as four times a year. A hundred other times it will pay off, but in minor, obscure ways—you made a catch easier than it otherwise would have been; you were there to pick up a ball beside or behind another fielder, but could have got there any-way.

Four times a year.

The difference, four times a year, can be (and has been) the difference between first and fourth place in the final standings.

The irony is that the more things you are skilled to remember, the more you may forget. A high school player who thinks of nothing except how many are out will seldom if ever forget that one fact. A major leaguer whose mind has computed as many as 40 different contributing elements before each and every pitch of a game is inevi-tably going to "lose" one from time to time—and will look like the rankest playground bumbler in the process.

But now, this afternoon in May, 1961, Lee Maye was leading off for the Braves.

He singled to right field.

Frank Bolling, the second baseman, followed, and flied to Felipe Alou in right. But Eddie Mathews singled, send-ing Maye to third, and now Hank Aaron homered over the fence in left, for three runs.

Marichal bowed his neck and struck out Joe Adcock, swinging. Frank Thomas hit one hard toward the hole, but Jimmy Davenport, the Giant third baseman, came up with the ball glove-handed and threw him out.

Davenport was the lead-off man for the Giants in their half of the first and drew a walk. Second baseman Charley Hiller lined the ball toward the wrong field, but Mathews, playing third for the Braves, speared it, and it became an easy double play on Davenport at first.

Now Mays stepped in. The count went to 3 and 2, and

then Bob Buhl, the Milwaukee pitcher, fired one hard across the outside corner. Mays had wanted the walk, to give McCovey and Orlando Cepeda a shot with somebody on base, but umpire Stan Landes said it was strike three.

The Braves went out in order in their half of the second inning. So did the Giants. In the top of the third, Maye, leading off for Milwaukee again, homered over the right-field screen, and with one out Mathews singled and stole second. But ground balls to Giant shortstop Jose Pagan provided the last two outs of the half-inning. The Braves led it now, 4–0.

That was enough for Dark. When Ed Bailey, the Giant catcher, worked Buhl for a walk opening the home half of the third, he decided to go for a pinch hitter for Marichal. Even when Pagan flied out for the first out, Dark stuck by his decision, and Matty Alou, Felipe's brother, hit for Marichal. And Matty walked.

Now Buhl got Davenport to pop to shortstop Roy McMillan, with the infield fly rule invoked. But Adcock at first muffed Hiller's grounder for an error, and the bases were loaded.

Mays was up, with two out.

The Giants had not yet had a hit off Buhl.

Willie took ball one, low; then fouled a curve ball, then took ball two, high and inside.

The next one was a fast ball, a little high, and Mays hit it. The ball tore on one soaring line beyond the bemused gaze of Aaron in center field and, on a deadly trajectory to the deepest reach of the ball park, on and out of there for a home run.

The score was 4–4.

Eddie Fisher came on to pitch the fourth for the Giants. Aside from a two-out double down the left-field line by

Charley Lau, the Milwaukee catcher, he escaped damage, and in the home half of the fourth the Giants went ahead 5–4 on singles by Felipe Alou and Bailey and an adroit squeeze bunt by Pagan.

In the Braves' half of the fifth, Fisher got Maye on a routine grounder to Hiller, and Bolling on a fly to Cepeda in left. But now Mathews got his third straight hit, a wrong-field homer to left, and when Aaron followed with a single, once again Dark made a move. He called in Stu Miller to do the pitching.

Miller personally retired Adcock on a bouncer back to the box, and with one out in the last of the fifth, with the score 5–5, Hiller, hitting to left once more, dropped in a double.

Up came Mays. Buhl threw two balls, then got a fast ball inside, and Willie wanted it. He swung and the thing went 16 rows up into the left-field stands. Now the Giants led 7–5.

McCovey homered for the San Francisco club in the last of the eighth, off Ron Piche, the third Braves pitcher (Buhl had vanished after that second Mays homer), to make it 8–5, and now there were two out in the ninth, with Miller having retired all 12 hitters he had faced so far.

Lau was the hitter, and he put up a Texas Leaguer back of second. Hiller went tearing out for it; Mays came rushing in. It seemed Hiller's ball, and at the last minute Mays swerved to avoid what appeared a certain collision.

So the catch was made, the game was over, and Mays, still running, headed for that right-field tunnel entrance— his shortest route to the Giant clubhouse.

Umpire Dusty Boggess was there to signal the final out, which he did.

But then Hiller turned around, his hands spread wide, his mouth open in disbelief.

He didn't have the ball.

Boggess did a take. Then he looked on the ground.

There was no ball there either.

Mr. Mays was in the clubhouse with it.

In the press box, veteran observers shook their heads, as if to clear them. Nobody had seen Willie catch the ball. But catch it he did.

"Well," said Don Davidson, the traveling secretary for the Milwaukee club, "we showed you how to handle Willie, didn't we? Keep him from running on the bases, I always say. Like we did today. Oh, I just love days like this!"

CHAPTER THREE

THE TERM SPECTACULAR

When, during the summer of 1962, the monthly *Diners' Club Magazine* decided to run a spread on the "most exciting athletes" in our different major sports, the editors went to *The Sporting News*, baseball's own weekly trade publication, for selection of the baseball candidate.

This was the result, as printed in the *Diners' Club Magazine:*

The term spectacular is synonymous with Willie Mays. It's as simple as that. Everything the brilliant San Francisco center fielder does reflects that aura.

Mays is probably the most spectacular player the game has ever seen. Mays can do so many things—run,

21

hit, catch, throw, slide—and do them with excitement. He is conceivably the only player who could lead the majors in just about every department: batting average, home runs, runs batted in, triples, doubles, total hits and fielding. He is the most natural player in action today.

Everything Mays does electrifies a crowd, whether it be running the bases like a runaway freight train that causes his hat to fly off his head, or simply catching a fly ball with that famous basket catch of his.

Mays plays the game with boyish enthusiasm. That is one characteristic that hasn't dwindled since he first put on a Giant uniform in 1951. Willie plays every game as if it were a World Series contest and never seems to tire in the process.

Perhaps the greatest tribute Mays receives is when rival managers and writers start comparing other ball players to him. That is a practice reserved for the great stars who have long retired. As usual, the comparisons fall way short.

Supposedly every player has his price tag. Not so in Mays' case. Six years ago, Cardinal owner Gussie Busch offered $1,000,000 cash for Mays, but was turned down without a moment's hesitation. St. Louis Cardinals' general manager Frank Lane learned in the process that there were some things which just had no price tag.

As San Francisco owner Horace Stoneham put it: "The name of the game is players, not money."

There is no greater name than Willie Mays.

In saying, *As usual, the comparisons fall way short,* the *Diners' Club Magazine* itself was falling short. It named categories in which Mays "conceivably" could lead the majors, without mentioning that in practically all of them, he already has. Indeed, the most startling tribute to Willie, statistically speaking, lies not in his individual talents, but in the ways he has combined these talents.

Nobody else, for instance, ever led his league in home runs and stolen bases, with more than 30 of each, in any one season. Mays has done it twice. Traditionally—and the figures support this—these are not only separate talents, but call for two different types of athlete.

This was nicely summed up by author Arnold Hano, when he wrote:

> Take the dreary year of 1960, when the wind blew from the Bay, toppling the Giants' chances and whirling (manager) Bill Rigney all the way to a rest home—the Rigneys'—in Oakland. Mays had himself—for him—a perfectly routine year. He hit .319, within two points of his lifetime average. In nearly every respect his performance was typically Maysian. He stole somewhat fewer bases than usual, but then there was a new rule in 1960. With Willie McCovey up, and Mays on first, the play was to stick near the bag, keep the first baseman close, and give McCovey a bigger hole to ram a ground ball through into right field.
>
> How did this routine Mays year rate with the rest of the league, statistically?
>
> Mays led his league in hits (190); was second in triples (12); third in batting (.319) and runs scored (107); fourth in runs batted in (103) and stolen bases (25); and sixth in doubles (29) and home runs (29). These are the eight offensive departments usually listed

in your newspaper and published throughout the season to afford more serious-minded Americans a constant source of heavy reading. In these eight departments, Mays had a first, a second, two thirds, two fourths, and two sixths. Figuring low score is best (first spot in any category is 1, tenth is 10), Mays' total in the eight offensive specialties is 29. Take a quick look, now, at some of the other fine hitters in the league. Dick Groat, selected the Most Valuable Player in the league, led the league in hitting and was second in total hits, but he was 13th in runs scored, 32nd in triples, 32nd in runs-batted-in, and he didn't steal a base all year. No contest.

Take a real slugger like Ernie Banks. Tenth in runs scored. Tenth in total hits. Fifth in doubles. Eleventh in triples. First in home runs. Third in runs batted in. Forty-fourth (among the regular hitters in the league) in stolen bases. Twenty-fifth in batting average (among hitters with at least 400 at-bats). Add 'em up. Remember, low score is best. Banks, 109; Mays, 29.

But, you say, Banks isn't fast. How about Henry Aaron? He can hit *and* he can fly. Aaron, 63, Mays, 29.

You can choose your hitter, and the same sort of result will obtain. Nobody in 1960 combined the various offensive abilities with such effect as Willie Mays.

And when you add to this the simple undenied fact that he is the finest fielding outfielder in the game, the totality of Mays' superiority in 1960—*a routine year for Willie*—over the best other players, is staggering.

Those who downgrade Willie—they are few, and becoming fewer, and most of the ones who are left are wholesale fans of somebody else (usually Mantle or the memory of DiMaggio)—have three talking points:

One—He's lucky. It's hard to say what this means, except that there are fans who believe it.

Two—He's favored by home-town scorekeepers. This can be answered. Such "favoritism," to begin with, can happen only, at best, some six to 12 times a year, crediting Mays with hits on balls that might possibly have been scored as errors. Again at best, or, if you like, at worst, this could not do anything grievous to any statistical category except Willie's batting average, number of singles, and runs batted in—a very small part of his overall credentials —and even those, it would hardly dent. One can also say it isn't wholly true that home scorers bend over backwards for him.

But the most cogent point is that for every home scorer who does favor Willie (though the charge cannot be proved), Mays and the Giants can point to a scorekeeper on the road who bends over the other way. And since Willie plays as much away as at home, this cancels out that. Period.

Three—He doesn't produce in the clutch.

This one's worthwhile examining. Many great players have heard this charge. The late Boston columnist Dave Egan hurled this accusation at the finest natural hitter of our time, Ted Williams. He found himself backed up by others, including, of all people, a Dr. David Tracy, who one year, as a gag, was hired as team psychiatrist for the St. Louis Browns, took his work seriously, and subsequently wrote a book in which he listed Williams as a prime example of a batsman who didn't hit well "under the gun."

This book has neither the background nor the purpose to turn psychiatric in the case of Willie Mays. But we can talk a little bit about the "clutch."

The San Francisco Giants had, in 1962, three games in which there was, literally, no tomorrow—a baseball fact without precedent.

Although there had been three previous postseason play-offs in the National League, not till 1962 did one of the two contending teams go into the last day of the regular season still trailing in the standings. That meant that for the Giants, a Dodger defeat was not enough. Merely to tie, the Giants had to win that final Sunday, even if the Dodgers did lose.

Win the Giants did, and lose the Dodgers did; and the postseason play-off then went the maximum three games, and the ensuing World Series the maximum seven games, a combination once more without precedent.

Here is what Willie Mays did in the clutch—his last time at bat in the final game of the season, his last time at bat in the final game of the play-off, his last time at bat in the final game of the World Series:

Sunday, September 30, vs. Houston. Score tied 1–1. None on, none out, last of eighth: *Mays homered.*

Wednesday, October 3, vs. Los Angeles. Giants trailing 4–2. Bases loaded, one out, top of ninth: *Mays singled.*

Tuesday, October 16 vs. Yankees. Giants trailing 1–0. Man on first, two out, last of ninth: *Mays doubled.*

Had enough of the "clutch"? Let us revert to statistics again, for a moment. There is one offensive statistic, prized by baseball men more than any other. That is the so-called slugging average. A batting average divides the number of hits by number of official times at bat. The slugging average does the same, but counts a double as two hits, a triple as three, a home run as four.

It is, therefore, a prime measure of the distance hitter. At the beginning of the 1962 season, Mays' lifetime slugging average was .585, tops among all active National Leaguers. At the end of the 1962 season, unofficial figures showed that .585 had moved up past .590, and therefore past Hack Wilson, the legendary Chicago Cub, to become the greatest lifetime slugging average of any National League hitter, past or present.

Well, you say, the real sluggers are in the American League?

One refers to the Introduction to Mays' autobiography *Born to Play Ball*, published in 1955, in which an interesting table appears. It compares the first full seasons of Mays' and five of the all-time great American League hitters—their first seasons in which they appeared in 125 games or more.

The slugging averages for those break-in years were:

Tris Speaker .443; Ty Cobb .473; Joe DiMaggio .576; Ted Williams .609; Babe Ruth .657.

And Willie Mays .667.

Time and again, however, it must be restated that neither figures nor the assertion of figures tell the story. Daniel M. Daniel, the most experienced baseball writer still active in his profession, said flatly, having seen them all, that Mays had the best throwing arm he ever saw. What figure tells this?

Bobby Bragan said, "If Mays is on the bench, you've got a chance." What figure tells this?

Charley Grimm said, "If Mays is on the bus with the rest of the team, you're in business." What figure tells this?

The four managers under whom Mays has played— Durocher, Rigney, Sheehan, Dark—have said flatly he is the greatest they ever saw.

Two late writers, Bill Corum and Jim Cruisenberry, both of whom saw Ruth, Cobb, Sisler, Speaker, Foxx,

DiMaggio, Williams, Musial—and all in their heydays—said Willie Mays was the greatest baseball player in history.

But the most important look at Mays was taken by a man whose opinion, nowadays, is not always quoted because he exists not in the headlines but behind the scenes.

"This was the greatest young ballplayer I had ever seen in my life," wrote Eddie Montague, in a private letter to Tim Cohane, the sports editor of *Look* magazine.

Since Montague was the scout who signed Willie in 1950, his reaction has meaning to Giant fans—which is putting it mildly.

A LETTER FROM MR. MONTAGUE

November 20, 1954

Mr. Tim Cohane
Sports Editor
Look Magazine
New York City, N.Y.

Dear Tim:

I have your letter of November 11, and I will try to give you a blow-by-blow account of the signing of Willie Mays.

In regards to Bill Maughn stating that he gave me my first tip on Willie Mays, I believe that he should correct his statement and say that he spoke about a young Negro ballplayer around Birmingham with a great arm, but I do not recall that Maughn ever mentioned the name of Willie Mays. However, that is beside the point, as I know it is a fact that Bill Maughn probably knew about Willie Mays before any other scout and I understand that he tried to get his organization to purchase the boy from the Birmingham Black Barons. I did not go in to see Willie Mays because Bill Maughn talked about him. The reason that I went into Birmingham was that, while at my home in Jacksonville, Fla., I received a call from our farm secretary, Jack Schwarz, to scout a player with the Birmingham Black Barons, named Alonzo Perry—a first baseman. This fellow had had a pretty good day in the Polo Grounds on the preceding Sunday and some of our scouts saw him and recommended him. I was told to scout Perry and see if he could help one of our Class A clubs. (Willie Mays may have played in the Polo Grounds also but no report was made on him.) The Barons toured through the Carolinas on their way back to Birmingham. One of our scouts picked up the club there and followed them into Birmingham. Still no report on Mays, who I know was with the club on this tour. When I arrived in Birmingham for the Sunday doubleheader I had no inkling of Willie Mays, but during batting and fielding practice my eyes almost popped out of my head when I saw a young colored boy swing the bat with great speed and power, and with hands that had the quickness of a young Joe Louis throwing punches. I also saw his great arm during fielding practice, and during the games his speed and fielding ability showed up. This was the greatest young ballplayer I had ever seen in my life or my scouting career.

During the ball games I moved around watching the action from different angles and saw most of the games from on top of the roof. It was here that I met Mr. Hayes, owner of the Barons. I asked him about the young center fielder and how much he was asking for the boy. He told

In 1951 Trenton fans attended a New York Giant game to present Willie with a painting of himself, among other gifts. Mays had formerly played for Trenton.

me $15,000 was the price, half now and half when the boy
reported, and also that he wanted to use Mays on his club
for the balance of the season. After the game I went down
to the locker room to meet Willie Mays. He had just
gotten out of the shower and I saw a well-built young
fellow. I talked with Willie for a few minutes and I was
impressed by his likable attitude. I told him I would see
him play the following night at Tuscaloosa, Ala.

I then went to my hotel and called Jack Schwarz at his
home and told him my report on Alonzo Perry, who I said
was not a major league prospect but o.k. for Class A. But
then I gave him my report on Willie Mays and asked him
if he had any reports on the boy. He said no, never heard
of him. I told Jack I would see Mays the following night
and if I still liked him I would try to purchase his contract
from Mr. Hayes.

I was at the ball park, in Tuscaloosa, very early the
following night. In fact, if it weren't for the groundskeeper I would have been lonesome. When the Barons
came in to the ball park I immediately cornered Willie
and asked him if he would like to play professional baseball, and he said, "Yes, sir," so I told Willie that I would
speak with Mr. Hayes about his contract. Willie said,
"What contract? Mr. Hayes don't own me," so I told
Willie if that were the case that I would deal directly with
him. I got his address and phone number at Fairfield, Ala.,
and told him I would call him the following morning.
The next morning I called and Willie told me that I
would have to speak with his Aunt Sarah, so I asked her
how much they wanted to sign a contract, and the answer
was $5,000. I told her I would contact my office and be at
their house that afternoon. (Incidentally, I felt that I had
to work fast, as I had seen Ray Blades, Brooklyn scout, in

the stands at Tuscaloosa, and I was sure that he was there to see Mays. Willie had a great night, hitting line drives to all fields and making a great catch and throw.)

I told my farm secretary that I could get Willie Mays for $5,000 and that he was not under contract with the Birmingham Black Barons. I told Schwarz that Mays would be playing center field in the Polo Grounds in two years, and Jack said, "If he's that good, go and get him." He also told me that I had better put a clause in the contract that Willie Mays was not orally or writtenly obligated to any other baseball club and then have it signed and notarized. Schwarz also asked me what classification Mays could start playing, and I suggested Class B so that he could get the feel of pro ball and gain confidence.

That afternoon I was at Willie's house in Fairfield. Willie's aunt and young sister were at the house, and about 4 P.M. Willie's father came home from the steel mill where he was employed. Mays senior was a former semi-pro ballplayer and he was a proud man that day when Willie signed his first contract. After talking about the Giant organization and professional ball and what I thought of Willie's chances of getting to the majors, I drew up the contract, and then Willie, his father, his aunt and young sister proceeded to a notary to have the contract signed and notarized. After I left the Mays' house I went directly to the post office and mailed the contract in, air mail special delivery. I then went to a drug store and called Jack Schwarz and told him that I had just signed a great young kid and that the contract was in the mail. At that time Jack Schwarz told me that we might have to pay Mr. Hayes something for Mays after all, as the Giant officials felt it was the right thing to do, so Mr. Hayes was sent a check for $10,000, which made everyone happy and also proves again and again what a grand organization the Giants are.

I understand that other clubs were interested in Mays at the time I saw him, but they were dealing with Mr. Hayes. We signed Mays and dealt with Mr. Hayes later, which in my opinion is the reason Willie Mays is playing for the Giants today.

These are all true facts in the scouting and signing of Willie Mays.

Sincerely yours,
s/ Eddie Montague

BORN TO PLAY BALL?

The idea that Willie Mays was "born to play ball" seems, to many people who watch him perform on the field, obvious at face value. Others believe that the fact that as a crawling infant, back in Alabama, Willie used to love to roll a ball at his father and cried every time the game was stopped, must mean Mays was, indeed, "born to play ball."

But, at the risk of seeming to change the subject for a moment, here is a story that appeared in the San Francisco *Examiner* in March of 1961:

Tucson, Arizona, March 19—Did he or didn't he? Maybe only the ball-park hairdresser—er, groundskeeper—knows for sure, and then only if he knows how to read a divot.

But one of the liveliest discussions ever to center around a play in an exhibition game continued far into the night and the next day as to Willie Mays' unbelievable nab of a sure two-run base hit in Saturday's Giants-Indians game here.

Mays said he caught the ball, and most of the Giants —and a couple of Indians—agreed.

Most of the Indians—and a couple of Giants—said he trapped it at grass-top level and conned umpire Frank Secory into calling the out.

"It was straight magic," a prominent Clevelander said. "You've got to give him that. One minute he's trapping the ball and seconds later he's holding it out and showing it in his glove, and the ball's so far out of the glove you say he couldn't have trapped it. He'd have had to catch it."

Muttered Indian manager Jimmy Dykes: "He didn't catch it. Why didn't I say anything about it? Because I know that umpire, that's why. What was the use?"

"He's still Willie Mays," said Cleveland coach Mel Harder. "He had his reputation going for him."

"I thought he caught it," Giant manager Alvin Dark said. He grinned. "What's the fuss about, anyway? It's routine for Willie." Then, thoughtfully, Dark pointed out: "If he doesn't catch it, then he comes up throwing the ball."

There might be a point there, for not only were three runners in motion, but the situation—with two out in the bottom of the sixth and the Giants ahead 2–1—was nothing if not critical.

Though the Giants went on to win, 4–1, there was no doubt that, as coach Salty Parker put it, "Mays saved us the ball game."

He also saved manager Dark from the first concerted second guess he would have had to defend against. For with two out and a man on second, Dark had ordered an intentional walk to Willie Kirkland—going against the book by putting the lead run on base in a late inning.

Runners moved up on a passed ball, and Jack Kubiszyn's sinking liner well to Mays' left was ticketed as a sure bet to score them both. Till Willie did what Willie did.

"The percentage didn't mean anything to me," Dark said later. "What's the difference if you go out to tell the pitcher don't give him anything good, or just go ahead and walk him?

"If you tell him go ahead and pitch, you might hear the sound of that base hit leaving the bat before you get back to the bench."

Further, said Dark, "In a case like that, I want the responsibility. My pitcher has enough worries of his own."

But Mays' catch—old-timers who have seen him in New York as well as San Francisco called it one of his all-time best—got everybody off the hook.

As to whether he actually caught it, two things can be said. First off, those who think he didn't may be possessed of logical minds that tell them the ball simply could not have been caught, regardless of what their eyes tell them. Unbelievable is surely a correct word for it.

And secondly, Giant pitcher Sherman Jones summed it all up in one short sentence:

"If he traps it, it's still a heck of a play."

The point in reproducing this story is to show the amount of interest that can be generated by a Mays play *in a game that means nothing*! It is here, perhaps, that best lies proof that here is someone who was born to play ball.

Not just that one, but a good half dozen of his most talked-about plays throughout his career have been things that happened in exhibition games.

In exhibition play, an established player can go all-out because he is trying to get in shape, or because he is battling for his job, or because rumors have it he may be traded, or for a few other assorted reasons—including the sheer joy of playing baseball. Since Mays has never had, in his entire baseball career, any of the specific worries outlined above, we had best look elsewhere—and that's where the sheer joy of it enters in.

"The best throw I ever saw *24* make," said Bill Rigney, "was in a tank town in Texas someplace, and don't ask me the name of the town. We were on our way back from training in Phoenix—on our way back to New York. It was either 1956 or 1957. Don't ask me that either. Anyway, we were touring with the Indians, and it was when Colavito was new to the league. I think it was Colavito—don't pin me down. No, it *was* Colavito. Anyway, *24* threw him out at the plate trying to score from first on a triple to left center. All right, now ask me how do you *not* score from first if it's a triple? Again, I don't know. All I do remember is that this particular left field didn't have any fence at all. Willie all but disappeared into the next county going after that ball. All I remember is—and this I *do* remember—he caught up with it, and here it came!"

Or take the 1962 pennant race, with its unbearable tensions—so furious they were that Mays had collapsed from exhaustion in the dugout at Cincinnati in mid-September. Then came the unbelievable race to the wire, the three games of the postseason play-off, the seven games of the World Series.

The day after the World Series, there was a story in the papers from Wichita, Kansas, where a postseason group of barnstorming American and National leaguers were playing each other. The Nationals won the game because one guy, who'd just flown in from San Francisco, hit a single and a home run.

Who was the guy?

24. Who'd you think?

Born to play ball?

You'd have to say so.

KITTY-KAT

Myth, both minor and major, has a way of catching on and holding on in baseball. One of the minor myths is that Willie Mays' full name is Willie Howard Mays, Jr. He is so listed in many texts, including the authoritative Little Red Book of Major League Baseball.

Mays' father was named William Howard Mays (he was born at the time William Howard Taft was President). But Willie Mays' full name is exactly that: Willie Mays.

Though he is not a "junior," he is a chip off the old block. Willie's father was a graceful semi-pro ballplayer. The father's father, Walter Mays, was a pitcher of repute in colored baseball in Tuscaloosa, Alabama, around the turn of the century.

One myth (the horrible thing is it's probably true) is that Willie was being scouted by a major league ball club at the age of thirteen! This of course points up an interesting fact about the letter from Giant scout Eddie Montague that makes up Chapter Four of this book.

Still no report on Mays, wrote Montague, even though he was only a couple of days away from signing him. Yet Montague sensed that Mays had already played in the Giants' own New York ball park, the Polo Grounds (that's true—he had).

Today, major league scouts get reports on ballplayers wherever and whoever they may be. But as recently as a dozen years ago, even after Jackie Robinson had broken baseball's "color line," colored baseball teams and leagues were still very much in business.

The truth, as it existed then, was that white scouts would accidentally run across talented colored players whose own reputation in their own leagues was known from one end of the country to another. Though Montague, one of the best scouts in the business, had not heard of him, Negro men from one end of the country to the other knew of the Birmingham boy who "come to play."

"Kitty-Kat's got himself a winner," they'd say. Kitty-Kat was the nickname hung on Willie's baseball-player father.

Mays himself was known as "Buckduck," a nickname that still remains (though usually now it is shortened to "Buck") when he grew to athletic prominence as a boy in Fairfield. Today, he cannot say why or how he got this nickname. Nor does he have outstanding memories of Fairfield, let alone the even smaller nearby community of Westfield, where he was born on May 6, 1931, the son of a tool worker in a nearby steel mill.

One story had it that Mays had to work as a child to

help bring in money in those depression times, but Willie
himself has said: "You can't ask me about the depression,
because I'm not old enough to remember much of it. Far
back as I can remember, FDR was already in his second
term. But I don't recall that we had any suffering. As far
as I remember, my dad always had work. We didn't have a
Cadillac, but neither did the people next door."

William Howard Mays—Kitty-Kat—was just eighteen
when Willie was born. Two years later, he and Willie's
mother were divorced, and Willie went to live with his
aunt Sarah—the wife of his father's brother—in a five-room
frame house in Fairfield. Mays has ten half brothers
and sisters by his mother's second marriage—one of the
brothers lives with him today in San Francisco—and even
though they did not live together then, they were, as
families go, quite close. Willie's mother died in November
of 1953 from complications arising from the birth of her
eleventh child, Diana. By then, Willie was long since
established as "the big brother."

At Fairfield Industrial High School, Mays is remembered as a triple-threat halfback in football, and he loved
the sport. Jim McWilliams, his high school football coach,
has told wild-sounding stories about Willie's prowess,
especially as a passer, and Mays' enthusiasm for the sport
cannot be denied. When he was thirteen, he shinnied up
a tree to watch Fairfield play Westfield in the big game
and, by his own account, "I got so excited I fell out and
broke my leg."

What is perhaps not so well remembered is that Mays
was an even greater basketball player. He led his county in
scoring in high school league play at the age of sixteen.

Occasionally, this combination is seen—the football
passer who also is a true star at basketball even though he

is not a tall man in a tall man's game. The outstanding example of this in big-time sports annals was Otto Graham, who for all his fame in football was, some experts claim seriously, truly one of the four or five greatest basketball players of all time.

Lynn Waldorf, Graham's football coach in college, had the explanation. "Along with his coordination as an athlete," Waldorf said of Graham, "he had what you call peripheral vision. It's the closest thing to having eyes in the back of your head. The great passers in football have to have it. And the great players in basketball, unless they're seven footers, have to have it."

There is a great deal of basic sense to this theory—not only is it basic, but it is vital. It is seen in Mays in the way time and again he avoids collisions with fellow fielders while seemingly intent only on the flight of the ball and, again seemingly, totally unaware of another man's presence.

Peripheral vision is hardly the whole story, but it is a tremendous plus, seldom accounted and seldom seen. That, however, was not what guided Willie into baseball as a career.

Kitty-Kat did that.

Kitty-Kat was an outfielder. His own father had been a pitcher, but Kitty-Kat was a realist. "I don't want 'em hitting home runs off of me!" he declared.

In turn, he was the one who suggested the outfield to Willie. This was one of three memorable pieces of advice that Willie was to hear from his father.

Willie liked to pitch, as a boy. Once, Kitty-Kat said to him, "You know, pitchers don't get to play every day." Willie thought about that.

Then, the summer he was fourteen, Mays pitched nine

innings for a local team in a sandlot game and wound up the day by hitting a home run. It was a hot day, and as he crossed home plate he found himself feeling dizzy.

"Outfield?" Kitty-Kat said to him.

"Outfield," Willie agreed.

There was another piece of advice from Kitty-Kat. Mays had been taking a course in dry cleaning at high school—his only outside work so far had been a short stretch of washing dishes in a Birmingham cafe—and one night he fell to discussing the future with his father.

"Just one thing," Kitty-Kat said. "Whatever you do, don't go down to the steel mills to work."

"It's not such bad work," Willie said.

"No," his dad said. "But once you're in it, you never get out."

The third piece of advice from Kitty-Kat was intended for himself.

The day Willie went up to the major leagues, Kitty-Kat hung up his spikes. He could have gone on playing sandlot and semi-pro ball himself.

"But I told myself," he has since recollected, "one in the family is enough."

"MY NAME'S DIMAGGIO!"

So Kitty-Kat was an outfielder, and Kitty-Kat's father before him was a pitcher. And even Willie Mays' mother, Ann, had been a running star herself, in girls' track meets.

So Willie had rightfully come by his athletic ability, and his father's example channeled that ability into baseball.

Something else happened too.

Willie was ten in the summer of 1941—the first year he began to take a true interest in baseball. And what fed that interest was a man named Joe DiMaggio.

Playing center field for the Yankees, the San Francisco-born DiMag was in the midst of what may go down as the most concerted hitting splurge baseball ever knew. He hit

safely in 56 straight games, and as the streak mounted it
became front-page news throughout the country—including Birmingham, Alabama.

Mays and his best boyhood friend, Charles Willis,
played catch in a vacant lot in Fairfield, day in and day
out that long lazy summer of 1941.

"Hey, DiMag!" Willis would yell out as Mays drifted
back to take one over his shoulder.

"That's me!" Mays would call back happily.

And it *was* him . . . to a point of wicked irony, years
later, when he found that some San Francisco fans resented
him as a threat to the fame of their own home-grown
center fielder, Joe D.

One time Mays was in that vacant lot all by himself,
running bases.

Kitty-Kat happened to pass by. He said, "Who are you?"

"DiMaggio," Willie said.

"Okay, DiMaggio," Kitty-Kat said. "What can you do?"

"Hit the ball. Throw the ball. Catch it. Run bases.
What else is there?"

"Picking it up," the Father said.

"Say what?"

"Picking it up," Kitty-Kat repeated. "Lots of things
come natural in baseball. Some things, you got to practice
on more than others. Picking it up is something you can
never practice enough. Let's start right now."

And from somewhere, a bat, ball and glove materialized,
and father and son began playing that time-honored baseball warm-up game called pepper.

Purposely, each time Willie threw the ball from 15 feet
away, Kitty-Kat would stroke the ball differently, mixing
the easy with the tough, the obvious with the unexpected.

"Pick it up!" he'd cry. "Pick it up! You're dug in like a potato plant! How can you go to the side? Bend those knees!"

In years to come, people would marvel at the way Willie Mays fielded ground balls in the outfield—at the way he would take infield practice with the scrubs before a game.

It came to be said of him that he "played center field like a shortstop." Which he did, and does. It is one of baseball's least-recognized ingredients. The fielding statistics don't show it. The infielder who gets a ground ball will show 95 percent of the time a put-out, assist, or error for his pains. Perhaps the one most common fielding chore an outfielder is called upon to perform is that same ball that has already hit the ground. He picks it up and throws it back. The fielding statistics will give him only an error if he boots it. He can't get a put-out on it. Once in a long while he'll get an assist.

But the assist by itself is no indication of a good outfielder, though many fans don't realize this. Baseball men will tell you that the outfielder with the most assists will generally be found under a combination of circumstances, none of them particularly desirable. It may be the other teams hit the ball to the outfield a great deal, and roll up the base hits. So you'll be throwing more but enjoying it less. The more men you throw on, the more assists you'll get. Or it can be that the other team is just plain running on you.

If they're running on you, it means they don't respect your arm.

In the World Series of 1954, an interesting thing happened. In the opening game, Giant right fielder Don Mueller threw *behind* a runner—a man who'd singled. As the hitter made his turn around first, Mueller faked the customary throw-in to second base, then, instead, whipped it back to first.

And it was a bad throw! It went past first baseman Whitey Lockman for an error, and the hitter got to second.

Commenting on that play afterwards, Willie Mays said:

"Don got an error for it. Maybe he should have got a medal."

For in that World Series, the Cleveland Indians went on to leave a total of 38 men on base in four games—and not one of them had made so bold as to even try to take an extra base.

Though by no means a bad fielder, Mueller was not the defensive equal of Mays in center or Monte Irvin in left.

The Indians may well have reasoned that if *he'd* try a play like that, what would those other two guys do?

And as Mueller's bad throw suggests, some outfielding skills are acquired. In Mays' case, sheer instinct—the instinct that Joe DiMaggio once said had to be there, could never be taught—was of course there from the start. So were the physical qualities—the speed, the strength of arm, the peripheral vision.

Some things, though, he learned through practice. Kitty-Kat was quite a teacher. Buckduck was quite a student.

And the matchless underground grapevine of Negro baseball soon got the word around:

"Kitty-Kat's got himself a boy there!"

When Willie was sixteen, his father said to him:

"Piper wants to talk to you."

Piper was Piper Davis, manager of the Birmingham Barons in the Negro National League.

Mays turned out for his tryout.

He stepped up to the plate in a warm-up game and took his stance. It was DiMaggio's stance he took, too; he'd seen pictures of the Yankee Clipper—and waited for the first pitch.

Standing there, he saw the pitcher release the ball.

Sitting there, he heard the umpire call it a strike.

He had been curved on the inside, and down he went.

Piper Davis called time and walked out to Mays at home plate.

"Know what pitch that was?" he asked.

"Curve," Willie said.

"Then why'd you go down?"

"I don't know."

"Would you like to know?"

"Sure."

"You were overcrowding," Davis said. "That's why. You don't stand on home plate and peer at the pitcher. You lay back and aim on him."

The education of Willie (DiMaggio) Mays had begun in earnest.

Years later, the word became common that Mays never had been taught a thing. Leo Durocher fed the reputation. "Who'd try to teach him anything?" he used to ask.

Mays himself got a kick out of that.

"When I started with the Barons," he has remembered, "I knew what my father had taught me and just about nothing else. Playing with the Barons taught me how much there was still left to learn. Finally, when I came to the Giants, I found out that in 20 years I just about hadn't learned a thing. My education really began when I got to the big leagues."

Then he began to laugh. "Now," he said, "every time I

read about myself, somebody's taking credit for how much he *didn't* have to teach me! Man, *somebody* had to teach me!"

A lot of somebodies did.

But there is still a firm plateau of truth in the Durochers who said they never had to teach Mays a thing. It is like the rules of baseball. Somewhere along the line, Willie had to learn them. He was in organized ball before he realized the rules say that in getting back to a base after, say, a long fly ball, you have to touch any bases you passed on the way. But he was already quite a ballplayer.

Maybe he himself expressed it best when, playing with the Birmingham Barons, he missed the team bus for an out-of-town trip and had to run to catch up with the rest of the players.

When he finally started to board the bus, manager Davis said, "Do you belong here?"

"Sure I do," Willie said.

"Why?"

"I'm a professional ballplayer."

"You are? What's your name?"

Willie grinned. "DiMaggio," he said, and got on the bus.

CHAPTER EIGHT

SIOUX CITY (ALMOST)

"The reason that I went into Birmingham was that, while at my home in Jacksonville, Fla., I received a call from our farm secretary, Jack Schwarz, to scout a player with the Birmingham Black Barons, named Alonzo Perry—a first baseman. This fellow had had a pretty good day in the Polo Grounds on the preceding Sunday and some of our scouts saw him and recommended him. I was told to scout Perry and see if he could help one of our Class A clubs. . . ."

So ran part of the letter from Eddie Montague which appears earlier in this story. The Class A club he was talking about was a Giant-affiliated team in Sioux City, Idaho.

Neither Perry nor the other fella (fella named Mays) ever made it to Sioux City. Willie Mays came close, though.

By the time Montague signed him, as we already know, Willie was a known figure among colored players. He had barnstormed with a team headed by Roy Campanella, already knew such future Giant teammates as Monte Irvin and Hank Thompson, and even, when he was seventeen, got to hit against the fabulous Satchel Paige.

Ballplayers remember moments like that.

Years afterward, Willie was asked whether he'd ever seen Paige.

"Hit against him," he said.

"Where?"

"I don't remember."

"When?"

"I don't remember."

"How'd you do off him?"

"One for two."

He obviously remembered the important part.

Willie remembered, too, the time in New Orleans when, playing in a barnstorming game for Campanella, he asked the famous catcher if he could play shortstop that day.

"I don't know why not," Campy said.

Mays recollects what happened then:

"I butchered the first ball that came my way. The second that came my way nearly butchered me."

From back of the plate, Campanella threw off his mask and hollered for time. "Change in line-up," he said to the umpire. "The shortstop will now play center field."

To Mays, Campanella said, "You asked me if you could

play short and I said I didn't know why not. Now I do
know."

The traveling days with colored teams were filled with
exciting moments for the young outfielder. An off day in
St. Louis gave Mays a chance to go Sportsman's Park—now
called Busch Stadium—and see the old St. Louis Browns
play the Boston Red Sox. He got a chance to watch Ted
Williams swing the bat.

"I just sat there with my mouth open," he confessed
afterward.

Another time, the Barons played at League Park, a
small, outdated ball yard in Cleveland where the Indians
of that era still played day games. They had already
switched to the mammoth Municipal Stadium, downtown
on the lakefront, for night and Sunday games. By the time
Mays next visited Cleveland—with the National League
All-Star team in 1954—League Park had been abandoned
entirely and all games were played at the Stadium.

Mays, though, was unprepared. "First thing I thought,"
he has recalled, comparing his 1954 visit there with the
one some years before, "was, man, did this place ever get
bigger!"

These things did happen. We say that because, with
such a star as Mays, myth is ever at war with fact, as we
have already seen. One story was that Tris Speaker, the
legendary center fielder of another era, saw Willie in a
barnstorming game and took him aside to give him some
special tips on how to play center field.

Some three years later, in 1954, somebody said to Willie,
"What did Tris Speaker actually say to you?"

"I haven't met him yet," Mays replied.

But myth stopped being myth shortly after Mays' high

school graduation. The Giants, who had hired him and (now that he was a high school graduate) could put him to work, sent him to their Trenton, New Jersey, farm team in the Interstate League. Chick Genovese was the manager there; the general manager was Bill McKechnie, Jr., son of the well-known former big league manager.

There was nothing mythical about Mays in his first 22 times at bat in the Interstate League. He went 0 for 22.

He went to McKechnie and said, "How am I going to hit this pitching?"

"You don't strike me as the worrying kind," McKechnie said.

"I'm not," Mays said.

"Then don't worry," McKechnie said.

So, in 81 games for Trenton in 1950, Willie wound up with a batting average of .353. He had 76 singles, 20 doubles, 8 triples, 4 home runs, 7 stolen bases, 55 runs batted in, 50 runs scored.

The next season Mays was promoted to Minneapolis of the American Association, class AAA—closest you can get to the big leagues.

In spring training at Sanford, Florida, Willie was introduced to a well-dressed, athletic-looking man.

"Maybe we'll meet again," the man said.

"Sure," Mays said.

And that was all there was to Willie's first meeting with Leo Durocher, manager of the New York Giants.

He didn't expect to see Leo soon again.

For that matter, he wasn't sure of his future with Minneapolis.

He went to Minneapolis manager Tommy Heath and said, "How am I going to hit this pitching?"

"Don't worry," Heath said.

So, in his first 35 games for Minneapolis in 1951, Mays had a batting average of .477.

And at that point, he was supposed to leave for Sioux City, for an exhibition game.

Willie was watching a movie in Minneapolis the night before the Sioux City trip when the theater manager interrupted the performance with a message that Mays should get in touch with manager Heath.

Mays went to Heath's hotel room, and the manager was holding out his hand and grinning.

"Congratulations!" he said.

"What for?" Mays wanted to know.

"You're going up to the big league."

"Who said so?"

"Leo."

"Not me," Willie said emphatically.

"What do you mean, not you?"

"I don't want to go to the big leagues."

"Why not?"

"How am I going to hit that pitching?"

Heath put his head between his hands. "Oh, boy," he moaned. Then he reached for the phone. "Here," he said to Mays. "You can tell Leo yourself."

Mays found himself talking long-distance to an impatient, angry Durocher.

"What do you mean, you're not coming up?" Leo yelled.

"I can't hit."

"What are you hitting now?"

".477."

There was a silence at the New York end of the phone.

Then, in a nearly broken voice, Durocher said huskily, "Can you hit .250 for me?"

"I can try."

"Then get on up here!"

CHAPTER
NINE

THE GIANTS' MOST
CRITICAL NEED

"The most sensational rookie ever to break into the big league." That is what Bruce Dudley, president of the American Association, said of Willie Mays when the Giants called him up from Minneapolis on May 24, 1951.

He had reason. That .477 batting average was only a small part of it. There were other things—the hole in the center-field fence at Milwaukee's old Borchert Field: Mays had put it there with a line drive. A group of fans suggested the hole be left unrepaired, as a memorial. The Milwaukee management agreed. (Years later, Milwaukee fans were to sympathize with Rip Repulski, then left fielder for the St. Louis Cardinals, when he explained how he caught a Mays drive against the fence at Busch Stadium: "I didn't exactly catch it. It kind of nailed me to the wall.")

And Mays himself.

Giant owner Horace Stoneham found himself in one of the most unusual predicaments in baseball history. He had to take out advertising space in the Minneapolis papers to try to cool down the fans. What came out was a straight apology, because the Giants had taken Willie away.

We appreciate his worth to the Millers [the ad ran], but in all fairness, Mays himself must be a factor in these considerations. Merit must be recognized. On the records of his performance since the American Association season started, Mays is entitled to his promotion, and the chance to prove that he can play major league baseball. It would be most unfair to deprive him of the opportunity he earned with his play.

We honestly admit, too, that this player's exceptional talents are the exact answer to the Giants' most critical need.

What was that most critical need?

It was a beaut—and not because the Giants were a bad ball club, but because they weren't. They had good pitching—the likes of Maglie, Jansen, Hearn; a fine catcher in Wes Westrum; the second base-shortstop combination of Stanky and Dark; and Lockman, Irvin, Mueller, Thomson —all top players.

They also had, for a manager, Leo Durocher, who is supposed to have said, "Nice guys finish last." That isn't what he said. What he did say was, "Nice guys finish second." You can see the difference, although, interestingly enough, Durocher couldn't.

It was not that he thought the club couldn't win, but that he thought it could, that had Durocher fuming.

The Giants, on the morning of May 25, 1951, were fifth in standings that looked like this:

	W	L	G.B.
Brooklyn	20	13	—
St. Louis	18	15	2
Chicago	17	15	2½
Boston	18	17	3
New York	17	19	4½
Philadelphia	16	18	4½
Cincinnati	15	19	5½
Pittsburgh	14	19	6

Obviously, they were better than they looked, not only on paper but with respect to the time of year. The standings in May are hardly an index. Take those third-place Cubs for example: they managed to wind up dead last with no trouble at all.

Furthermore, when Mays joined them, the Giants had won 15 of their past 22 games, which is pennant percentage to spare.

They had a bad start in the 1951 season. They won their first game, lost their second, won their third, then lost 11 straight. Even in that losing streak, though, they did not play badly, nor did they act disorganized or give every other ball game away. Even a pennant-winner will lose five in a row at one point, six in a row at another. The pennant-winning Yankees had a losing spell of nine straight in 1952. In the Giants' case it was just that the defeats were concentrated—all the balls bounced wrong at once.

Luckily, it happened at the very beginning of the season. A team that loses them then has time to recover. On the other hand, it had better not hit another losing pocket—unless it can afford to.

Afford to? What does that mean? It means not so much *how*, but instead *where*, you are in the standings. What Durocher didn't like about those standings was not his team's ability or performance, but the place the Giants were "laying" in the race. All other things being equal, including numbers of games left to play, we can make the hypothetical assertion that a big league manager would rather be in second place four games out of the lead than in fourth place two games out. This is because the higher you are in the standings, the more your destiny lies in your own hands. The only game you control is the one you're playing. If you're in fourth place and win, only to see all three clubs ahead of you win their games that day too, you not only haven't gained ground—you've actually lost it. For you stood still in the standings that day and now the season's one day shorter.

Playing talent? You can always use talent. But this was not the Giants' most critical need that moment in late May of 1951.

What they needed was something else. Call it anything you like—it's hard to put into words, really—an inspiration, a spark, a big moment.

"What," Durocher was asked afterward, "was it your club most needed at that time?"

Leo grinned. "What we most needed at that time," he said, "was Willie Mays."

GOOD-BYE!

Wrote Mays in his autobiography, *Born to Play Ball:*

I joined the Giants in Philadelphia on May 25, 1951. We were playing the Phillies that night at what was then Shibe Park (since that time, it's been renamed Connie Mack Stadium). Some of the Giants—Monte Irvin and Henry Thompson—I already knew, and of course, I'd met Durocher briefly in Florida.

But all of them had heard about me—thanks in the main to the New York press, which in the week previous had given me quite a build-up. I don't think all this, by any means, was caused by me. The Giants had started very slowly, and when you have a team that should be

playing better than it is playing, then you're liable to
hail any newcomer as the one fellow to untrack the ball
club and set it going.

I met the other players only briefly that first day.
Eddie Stanky, playing second base, said to me, "How do
you run the bases?"

"I don't know," I said. "I guess I could be better."

"Watch him," he said, and pointed across the clubhouse at Monte Irvin. "He'll show you some things. Last
game we played, he stole home."

"That's pretty good," I said.

"*Pretty* good?" Stanky said. "He stole home on a left-
handed hitter!"

I think that was just about the first of the little things
I've learned about baseball since I came to the majors
. . . that nine times out of ten, a man who steals home
does so only when there's a right-handed hitter at bat,
because then the batter's body blocks the catcher's view.

Strange to say, though, it was a little thing that did the
job for Willie—and the Giants—that first game.

The *New York Times'* story of the game next morning:

"Inspired by the presence of their flashy rookie star,
Willie Mays, the Giants rallied for five runs in the eighth
inning. . . ."

Mays went 0 for 5 at bat that day. He ran into teammate
Irvin in the field, and what should have been a fly ball
went instead for a double.

The little thing?

The little thing was that the Giants won.

Next day they won again, 2–0. Mays? Nothing.

Next day they won again, to sweep the Philadelphia
series. Mays? 0 for 4.

Fleet-footed Willie shows why you always "run it out." The Chicago Cubs' first baseman doesn't quite catch a poor throw from the infield and Mays is safe on the error.

So in his first 12 times at bat in the big league, Mays had a total of no hits.

As a result, the Giants had climbed over the .500 mark in the standings!

What did Willie have?

Writer Arnold Hano came up with one word to describe it.

"Quicksilver," Hano wrote. "That's what it was. Quicksilver."

But there was something else, too, as Hano has pointed out:

New York was exactly the right place, and 1951 the right time, for Willie Mays. Not only because of the color of his skin. Ball clubs have historical personalities. In New York there were three clubs. The Yankees—cold, remorseless, colorless perfectionists; the Dodgers—boisterous, bragging, bully-boys; the Giants—and the Giants were not used to losing. In the first half-century through 1950, Giant teams had won 13 National League pennants. They had won them, in fact, during the first 37 years of the century. In those 37 years, before the Giants started losing with the dreary regularity of a ticking clock on a bedroom wall, no team had won more often. . . .

Over that period, the New York Giants were baseball's finest team, swifter, more powerful, smarter, fiercer than any other. Now the club's personality lay like clay, like unmolded dough: dormant, dull, dispirited. . . .

The Giants were waiting, in 1951, for Willie Mays. On no other club—not even the Dodgers, where he might have hit 50 home runs every year in that perfectly tailored bandbox—was he so wanted, needed, hoped for, waited for.

Spark? Inspiration? Quicksilver?

Whatever it was, the Giants were back over .500 now, and they came back to the Polo Grounds to open a home stand against the Boston Braves, and the great Warren Spahn was pitching for the visitors.

Mays was batting third in the Giant batting order.

That night game of May 28, 1951, was one of beautiful weather, and a good crowd was on hand. They were there, for the main part, to see the new boy from Minneapolis.

A few of them noticed one rather strange thing.

In batting practice, Mays, with his DiMaggio-copying stance, reminded them in a way of the old Giant pitching immortal Carl Hubbell.

In the clubhouse between batting and fielding practice that night, manager Durocher brought it up.

"Hey, Hubbell," he said to Mays.

Mays said, "You talking to me?"

"Yes. You remind me of Hubbell."

"Why?"

"Because of the way you wear your pants."

"What's wrong with how I wear my pants?"

"You wear them down around your ankles."

It was true. Mays did wear the legs of his uniform trousers all the way down, with no bunching or slack below the knees.

"Well," he said, "if it was good enough for Hubbell, I guess I can do it."

"I wouldn't if I were you."

"Why not?"

"Because he was a pitcher. You're a hitter. You give the umpire too much of a strike zone."

Another little thing—Willie had never thought of it. The strike zone is supposed to start at the knees. If you wear your pant legs long and smooth, the umpire may make a mistake and think a pitch below the knee was actually just at the knee.

So when Mays took batting practice that night, his pants legs were down around his ankles. When he re-emerged for fielding practice, they had been hoisted up with more bunching around the knees.

A little thing? Certainly. Even less than little for something for the casual fan to have observed. What the fan wanted to do was see whether Willie would ever get a hit.

He was 0 for 12, remember.

So, his first time up against Spahn that night—it was with two out, nobody on, in the home half of the first—he saw a fast ball riding in at him, maybe a trifle high, but only a trifle.

Willie swung.

The Giants' long-time radio broadcaster, Russ Hodges, has a phrase he uses to describe any Giant home run. *"Bye-bye baby!"* he carols, and you know it's gone.

And here Mays swung, and there the ball went, on a rising, continuing line, up over the roof of the second deck in left field at the Polo Grounds. When last seen, the ball was still going up.

And a funny thing happened with announcer Hodges. He didn't say "Bye-bye baby!"

He didn't have time.

All he had time to say was, "Good-bye!"

THE SPIRIT OF '51

So Willie Mays had his first hit—a tremendous, walloping home run, far out into the night, off no less a pitcher than Warren Spahn.

So everything was fine.

Well, not quite.

In his next 13 times at bat, after the homer against Spahn, Willie again went hitless.

He went to Leo Durocher. Just as he had gone to McKechnie, just as he had gone to Heath. And said the same thing:

"How am I going to hit this pitching?"

The other two, McKechnie and Heath, had told him to stop worrying.

Durocher was even more direct.

"You're my center fielder," he said.

And Mays, hitting .039, went out and got nine hits in his next 24 times at bat. He broke out of the slump with a single and a triple as the Giants beat the Pirates, 14–3. Then in a game against the Cardinals he got two doubles and scored the only run in a 1–0 Giant victory.

The Giants were in third place.

Against the Cincinnati Reds, Mays got his second homer. In another game against the Reds, he batted in three runs. Late in June, on one road swing, Mays hit a three-run homer in the tenth inning at Chicago, went on a ten-game hitting streak, totaled four homers and 16 runs batted in for the road trip.

The Giants were in second place.

Back home again, Mays tied a game in the last of the ninth with a homer (Whitey Lockman homered to win it in the tenth). Of six hits he got late in July, all six were home runs.

On August 11, the Giants, in second place, had won 59, lost 50, meaning that since Mays had joined the club they had won 42, lost 31. And that's just what the Giants had made it—good, solid, second-place performance. No worse. No better.

The first-place team? Those Dodgers were so far in front you needed a tracing service to find them.

The Giants lost to the Phils, 4–0, on that August 11, while the Dodgers were beating Boston 8–1 in the first game of a double header. At that point, the top of the National League standings read:

	W	L	G.B.
Brooklyn	70	35	—
New York	59	51	13½

What was it Durocher had said? "Nice guys finish second. . . ."

But Leo had a feeling.

In a game earlier that week, the Dodgers had clobbered the Giants, and Brooklyn's great Jackie Robinson had added insult to injury by squeezing home an unnecessary added run in the ninth.

"The Dodgers really poured it on, don't you think?" Durocher was asked after that game. "Bunting on you that way when they didn't have to?"

"I'm glad they did," Durocher said.

"Glad?" he was asked.

"Sure," he said. "They got a run they didn't need, but while they were at it I stole their bunt sign!"

And Pee Wee Reese, the Dodger shortstop who had played under Durocher, was asked what he was going to do with his World Series money.

"We've still got to beat the Giants for the pennant," he snapped.

"You mean," he was asked, "with a 13½-game lead you're still worried?"

"You said it," Reese nodded.

But nobody paid any attention to him.

The Giants, least of all. Or so it seemed.

They beat the Phillies three straight now, winning 3–2, 2–1, and 5–2. Then, back home at the Polo Grounds, they won 4–2 over the Dodgers in the opener of a three-game series between the crosstown archrivals.

The next day they were tied with the Dodgers 1–1, with Brooklyn threatening in the top of the eighth inning. One was out, Carl Furillo—a good hitter—at bat, and Billy Cox —a fast runner—on third base.

Furillo now hit a fly ball of no more than medium

depth, but he hit it to right-center field, well to the left of center fielder Mays. Cox was tagged up, ready to go on the catch, and it seemed he would make it easily, for Mays, a right-handed thrower, could hardly get anything on a throw to the plate while traveling to his own *left*. Try it yourself. Your body gives you no momentum for a throw when you are traveling sidewise and away from the direction the throw must take.

So Willie Mays had a problem.

He solved it in a rather fantastic way.

He knew he couldn't throw Cox out via the routine method of catching and throwing.

So, as he made the catch, he came down on his left foot. Now, using that left foot as a pivot, Willie swung around to his left so that for a moment he was facing the bleachers in deepest center field. Still pivoting, he completed the circle. And came out of it throwing to home plate—this time with, obviously, *momentum* back of the throw. Again, try it yourself.

Cox was out at home.

Charley Dressen, the Brooklyn manager, was asked what he thought about that play.

"I can't tell you," he said.

Why not? he was asked.

"Because," Dressen said simply, "he'll have to do it again before I'll believe it."

Whitey Lockman, at first base, had lined himself up in between Mays and home plate to give Willie a "bead" on his throw. This was an automatic move on Lockman's part, rather than any kind of cut-off play, because there was nobody to cut off. The only runner was Cox going for the plate. But the maneuver served Willie's aim in good stead, and after the game, Lockman said to manager Durocher: "What would you have done if I'd cut that throw off?"

Durocher's reply is not printable.

Time magazine came out afterward referring to that play simply as "The Throw." That sounds a little too much, but that's what they called it.

Anyway, it was a great one—and a double play, and the Giants were out of the inning.

Mays, writing in his autobiography some years later, had this to say about what followed "The Throw":

> I suppose you've noticed how often a man who makes a big play in the field is first up at bat in the next inning, and how often the big play seems to be the last play of the inning. Well, maybe there are a couple of reasons for that seeming to be so. One of the reasons is that one of the things that helps make a play a big play is often that the play gets you out of the inning. The other is that if the man who made it isn't first up when his side comes to bat, the fans usually overlook it. When I was a kid in Alabama, I had a friend who lived close to the railroad tracks, and he was forever saying how this express train was always late. Fact was, it was late maybe two or three times a month, but he never paid it any mind when it was on time.

Be that as it may, Willie was first up for the Giants in the last of the eighth, following "The Throw." The crowd thundered and volleyed in joy and admiration. Promptly, Willie singled.

And Wes Westrum homered, and the Giants won it, 3–1.

Then, on a Maglie four-hitter, they beat Brooklyn 2–1 to sweep the Dodger series.

Then they beat the Phils 8–5, 2–0 (with Jansen out-pitching Robin Roberts) and 5–4. In that 5–4 game they scored five runs in the seventh to overcome a 4–0 Philadelphia lead.

Now the western clubs came into the Polo Grounds. Cincinnati was the first customer. The Reds led 4–2 going into the last of the eighth. It could have been 5–2, except for a Mueller-Mays-Lockman-Westrum relay from deepest right-center in the top of the seventh to cut down Hank Edwards of Cincinnati as he tried to stretch a triple into an inside-the-park home run. So it was a 4–2 lead for Cincinnati instead of a 5–2 lead, but it could have been a 5–2 lead. Either way, the Giants would have won the game. They scored five times in the last of the eighth, on homers by Stanky, Lockman and Westrum. Westrum's came with two men on base.

Next day the Giants defeated the Reds, 4–3. The Cardinals came in for a single game and led 5–4 going into the last of the ninth. The Giants scored twice and won it, 6–5.

They'd won 12 in a row and coming up were four games with the Cubs.

The four took the form of two consecutive double headers.

The Giants swept the first one, 5–4 and 5–1.

In the first game of that second double header, the score was tied at 3–3 going into the top of the twelfth. The Chicago team got a run to lead 4–3. In the last of the twelfth the Giants scored twice and won 5–4.

The second game of that twin bill? Giants 6, Cubs 3.

The Giants had won 16 games in a row. In the process, they'd cut eight full games off Brooklyn's league lead.

There was still a long, long way to go. But Arch Murray, a New York sports writer, said, "Those Giants are going to do it!"

How did he know?

"The spirit of '51," he replied. "Just you wait and see."

"WHAT IF IT'D BEEN ME?"

The Giants didn't win all their remaining games in 1951. In one of them they lost, in fact, Willie Mays forgot to touch third base while running out an inside-the-park home run (embarrassing, but not critical—that run didn't mean the ball game one way or another; eleven years later, in San Francisco in 1962, he was to wander off third thinking three were out when there were only two out, again during the end of the pennant race and again in a game the Giants lost—and again, embarrassing, but not critical. Does Mays make mistakes? Yup.)

No, the Giants didn't win all their remaining games in '51, but they sure won their share. In a never-to-be-forgotten final week ("They're closing the Brooklyn

Bridge—at both ends," wrote sports writer Howard Sigmand) they came down to the final day of the season tied with the Dodgers for first place.

The Giants beat the Braves that final day, 3–2. Brooklyn was losing badly to Philadelphia, but Jackie Robinson pulled it out twice for the Dodgers, once with a great catch, again with a home run, both times in extra innings.

So there'd be a play-off—the second in National League history.

For the regular 154-game season, both the Giants and Dodgers had won 96, lost 58. For the Giants since that fateful August 11th when they stood 13½ games behind, that meant they had won 37 of their last 44 games!

The Dodgers, over the same period, had won 26 out of 49—better than .500 baseball! Anyone who remembers that the Dodgers "folded" in 1951 is remembering wrong!

That 16-game winning streak, of course, played the big part in the Giants' 37-out-of-44 pace, but that was by no means the whole story. The Giants also won 12 of their final 13 games, and their last seven in a row.

In baseball, "miracles" are accomplished in all sorts of different ways. The traditional "miracle" was the Boston Braves of 1914, who came from last place on July 4 to win the pennant. But those Braves were in first place at the beginning of September. This does not lessen what they did. Their performance did, however, lack the "stretch" ingredient.

Since then, many teams have overtaken many other teams in the final weeks. These were exciting pennant races, but not "miracles."

Since the Braves of '14, in fact, three things have happened that qualify for that "miracle" label:

One—In 1951, a team that was 13½ games behind on August 11 came on to win the pennant.

Two—In 1954, a team that had finished in fifth place the year before, 35 games out of the lead, won the pennant by five games—a swing of 40 games' difference in the "games behind" column in the space of one season.

Three—In 1962, a team that trailed by four games with seven games left to play *won the pennant!*

Those, gentlemen, are miracles. One after another. And compared to those three performances, the "miracle" Braves of 1914 looked pale.

The interesting thing is that, in the case of all three "miracles," it was the Giants who won. As a matter of fact, going back what is now more than a quarter of a century, those are the only three pennants they have won in that period of time.

All three times, their center fielder was Willie Mays.

He is, in fact, the only active player on all three of those pennant-winning teams.

The point being made here, though, is the different ways pennants can be won—even within the framework of the miraculous.

The '62 pennant was won staggering. The '54 pennant was won breezing. The '51 pennant was won in such a roaring, concerted stretch run (baseball has never seen its like, before or since) that the Giants literally created new fans as they went along. People who'd never paid attention to baseball before found themselves picked up and swept along by the sheer drama and momentum of the Giant drive.

By the time the first play-off game was ready to take place at Ebbets Field, the whole country was watching.

It would be hard to top what the Giants had done already.

History records, though, that Leo Durocher's club found a way.

They beat the Dodgers 3–1 in that opening play-off game. Jim Hearn pitched a five-hitter. Monte Irvin, who'd hit 23 homers during the season and who led the league in runs batted in with 121, homered off Brooklyn's Ralph Branca. Earlier, Bobby Thomson, who had hit 30 homers in the regular season and batted in 101 runs, cuffed that same Branca for a two-run homer.

Mays, who'd had 20 home runs for the year—not bad for a youngster, comparing his season's total with those of Irvin and Thomson and remembering that Willie had missed the first quarter of the season—was not doing much in the play-off. He hadn't been doing much all of September, if you go by statistics. (The statistics show, for instance, that he stole two bases in one game at Boston. They don't show that he stole second and third in order, then came in to score the winning run on an infield grounder.)

Anyway, nobody on the Giants did much that second game of the play-off at the Polo Grounds. The Dodgers "danced at their own funeral," as one writer put it, winning 10–0 behind a newcomer named Clem Labine.

So it came down to a third and last game of the play-off, again at the Polo Grounds, Wednesday, October 3, 1951, and with only the last half the ninth remaining to be played, the twin scoreboards in right and left fields told the same story:

Brooklyn	1	0	0	0	0	0	0	3	0
New York	0	0	0	0	0	0	1	0	

This is how Mays, writing in his life story *Born to Play Ball*, sets the stage for what happened then:

> Monte Irvin and I were the last ones into the dugout from the field as the teams changed sides, left and center fields being the farthest away from the Giant dugout at the Polo Grounds. Usually by the time I got in to the bench from center field, Durocher already was on his way out to the third-base coaching box.
>
> This time, though, he was standing on the dugout steps, waiting till everybody got in.
>
> Then he turned around and faced us, leaning in on us with one hand up on the roof of the dugout, and looking from one face to the next. I never saw a calmer-looking guy.
>
> "Well," he said, sort of reflectively, "you've come this far. It's an awful long way to come. And you've still got a chance to hit." And then he went on out to the coaching box, with that number 2 still looking big and jaunty on his back.
>
> Alvin Dark led off for us and slapped a hard grounder to the right side. Second baseman Jackie Robinson and first baseman Gil Hodges scissored across, Robinson the deep man, and for an instant we couldn't tell what would happen. But the ball was through between them and into right field for a single.
>
> Now Don Mueller stepped in. He hit an almost identical shot—a little more to the right, maybe, but Hodges was playing him over that way, so the difference was the same. Again Robinson gave it the deep try and again the ball was through. Dark stopped at second, taking no chances with the score 4 to 1 against us in the last of the ninth.

Irvin, our big hitter, came to bat now. Out in the Dodger bull pen, three pitchers were working like crazy. A home run now—well, it was crazy even to think about it, but it would tie the score.

But Monte put up a meek foul fly to the right side, and there was one out. You should have seen the way Irvin slammed that bat down. He was sick over it.

That brought Lockman to bat. And for the third time in the game he sliced a double to left field. This one zipped past Cox at third. Dark tore around to score from second. Mueller, facing a potential play at third, slid so hard into third base that he sprained his ankle— so severe a sprain that he had to be carried from the field on a stretcher.

Red Smith wrote in his column the next day that the scene at that point—stretcher bearers—seemed the perfect final touch.

Clint Hartung went in to run for Mueller, so he was leading off third, Lockman off second, as Bobby Thomson stepped to the plate. We were behind 4 to 2 now, with one out and the tying runs both in scoring position. . . .

Any number of concentrated second guesses have swirled ever since around what happened next. Obviously, the Dodgers needed a new pitcher to replace their tired ace, Don Newcombe. Should it have been Branca, who had thrown a home run ball to Thomson two days ago, or someone else? ("My bull pen coach said Branca was the sharpest," said Brooklyn manager Dressen.) Should the Dodgers have pitched to Thomson or put him on, loading the bases for a possible force or double play and getting rid of that hot long bat in the Giant order? ("That would have meant putting the winning run on base for the home team in the last of the ninth," said Dressen, "and you never do that.")

Anyway, you all know what happened.

Branca did come in, and the Dodgers did have him pitch to Thomson.

Not only second-guessing, but mythology also enters here—were there two out? No, there was only one out. Did Campanella, the Brooklyn catcher, call for the wrong pitch? Campy wasn't doing the catching. Did Thomson hit the first pitch? No, the first pitch was a called strike ("a better pitch," plate umpire Lou Jorda said afterward, "than the next one.")

That next one was a fast ball, a little inside.

Thomson wanted it.

He swung.

The ball tracked out in a low arc toward left field.

Andy Pafko, the Dodger left fielder, planted himself against the 12-foot wall there and waited.

But it was gone.

There have been great, climactic moments, before and since (most of them, but not all, rightfully enough in play-off or World Series games, when the chips are down and there's no tomorrow). There was the ball that hopped over Lindstrom's head in 1924 in that Senators-Giants Series finale that down through the ages is the best-remembered *game* (as opposed to that final moment) in baseball annals. There was Gabby Hartnett's "home run in the gloaming" for the Cubs in '38. There was Cookie Lavagetto's last-minute double to spoil Bill Bevens' no-hitter in '47, and there was the last pitch of Don Larsen's perfect game in '56. There was, certainly, Bill Mazeroski's Series-winning homer for the Pirates in '60.

But none of them—no, none of them, not even that same October 3rd eleven years later when once again the Giants scored four runs in the ninth inning to come from behind and win a play-off finale against the Dodgers—hold a candle to that moment in 1951.

The setting was there, the rivalry was there, everything was right. But most of all was what Leo Durocher told his Giants: *"You've come this far. . . ."*

This is how Red Smith, finest sports columnist of our day, began his story the next morning:

> Now it is done. Now the story ends. And there is no way to tell it. The art of fiction is dead. Reality has strangled invention. Only the utterly impossible, the inexpressibly fantastic, can ever be plausible again.
>
> Down on the green and white and earth-brown geometry of the playing field, a drunk tries to break through the ranks of ushers marshaled along the foul lines to keep profane feet off the diamond. The ushers thrust him back and he lunges at them, struggling in the clutch of two or three men. He breaks free, and four or five tackle him. He shakes them off, bursts through the line, runs head-on into a special park cop, who brings him down with a flying tackle.
>
> Here comes a whole platoon of ushers. They hit the man and haul him, twisting and kicking, back across the first-base line. Again he shakes loose and crashes the line. He is through. He is away, weaving out toward center field, where cheering thousands are jammed beneath the windows of the Giants' clubhouse.
>
> At heart, our man is a Giant too. He never gave up.

Willie Mays' recollection of that moment?

"My greatest thrill," he said afterward.

And years later, he added thoughtfully:

"You know, I was in the on deck circle, next due up at bat, when Thomson hit it. I was just a kid then. What if it'd been me?"

THE *REAL* DIMAGGIO

The day following Bobby Thomson's "home run heard round the world," the 1951 World Series began: Giants vs. Yankees, at Yankee Stadium. And, of course, no one had eyes for anyone but Thomson. Much as he had provided the spark that took the Giants to the pennant, it had been Thomson who nailed the flag to the mast, and others who headlined the September drive, and Mays was best known at this moment for what he'd said to Monte Irvin in Boston that final Sunday of the regular season.

It was a laugh line, though Willie wasn't laughing when he said it. What had happened was that the last out of the Giants' final victory over the Braves had come on a routine fly ball to Irvin in left. As Monte camped under the ball,

Mays came charging full tilt from center field, shouting as he came.

A couple of days later, somebody thought to ask Irvin what it was Mays was yelling as he ran.

"All he said," Irvin grinned, "was: 'Catch it. Catch it or I'll kill you!'"

This story is of interest now because it presents a stunning contrast to the Mays of 1951 and the Mays of ten years later. Once in 1961, the Giants were playing a night game at Los Angeles, and the first innings of such night games, which begin at 8 P.M. Pacific Coast time, can be tough on outfielders, who "lose" the ball in what is left of the twilight at that time.

Maybe you know that left-handers earned the nickname of "southpaw" because when they take their pitching position on the mound, their left arm is toward the south. All major league, and most minor league, ball parks are laid out this way, for the simple reason that such a layout keeps the sun out of the batter's eyes.

Night games that start at 8 P.M. on the coast, however, can be awfully tough on the fielders—particularly the right fielder, who is looking directly into the west, where the daylight still remains.

So it happened, this night in 1961, that Felipe Alou, the Giant right fielder, simply lost a fly ball headed for right field. Mays, with a bead on it, and knowing the sky background for what it was (part of his routine "checklist," as outlined in Chapter Two of this book), was off at the crack of the bat. So it was that Willie Mays, the center fielder, made the catch in dead right field, a full 50 feet behind his right-fielder teammate.

The Mays of 1951 might have usurped another player's

ball because he didn't know any better. The Mays of 1961 did the same thing because he *did* know better! The physical ability to be in another man's territory was the same in '51 as in '61—and few outfielders can travel that far in that short a space of time in any event.

The skill was one thing. The knowledge of how, when, and whether to apply it is something else. Yet this is certainly not the same discussion we had earlier in this story, about the things Willie was taught. Being taught is one thing, learning by yourself is another.

And this, largely, is what Willie Mays means today when he says, "I didn't know anything when I came up to the big league." It is true that he learned. But in several main respects, he was his own teacher. He learned by doing—and by watching.

And, perhaps unconsciously, he modeled himself after the one other truly great center fielder of our time—Joe DiMaggio.

DiMag and Mays shared two things that old-timers say no other center fielder in history, not even the legendary Speaker, or Terry Moore, or Joe D.'s brother Vince DiMaggio, would exhibit. Mickey Mantle said once it was one of the things he admired the most in DiMaggio—and something he (Mantle himself) wished wistfully that he could acquire.

You can compare DiMag and Mays only up to a point, for over their careers, Joe and Willie had, by and large, different quality performers in right and center fields, and the edge, frankly, would have to be on DiMaggio's side. DiMag played with established Yankee stars, not the least of whom was Tommy Henrich, one of the unsung defensive greats of all time in right field. Mays' very ability to cover ground emboldened Giant managers to sacrifice defensive strength in right or left fields—sometimes both, as in a game in 1961 in which manager Alvin Dark flanked Willie with Orlando Cepeda (by his own admission a borderline case in the outfield) in right and catcher Ed Bailey playing left in his first big league outfield assignment.

The point is that DiMaggio and Mays both came to acquire a built-in *knowledge* not of how to go beyond their own positions, but *when* to! And in Mays, this is a particularly interesting thing. Ten years ago he didn't know how to apply this knowledge. Five years ago, he knew how, and every time he sensed a fellow fielder was in trouble, he was by his side to help out.

Today, Willie can still be by his side—and just as fast as always—but he will do so less often. If the right fielder's going to have trouble with a ball, Willie will be there only if the overall situation demands it! But if the score's 10–2 in the last of the eighth—regardless of who's ahead—don't look for Willie. He won't be there.

Is this "quitting"? No, it's far less a crime than that, and far more sophisticated. Willie can make the same play today that he could make five years ago—but not if he makes it as often. So, very basically, he does it when it counts—and he's skilled enough to sense unerringly when those "count" occasions are there. Other times, he'll save himself.

Joe DiMaggio did the same thing in the closing days of his career. They say the legs are first to "go" on you, but with DiMag it was the arm.

DiMag still could throw as brilliantly as ever, but it got to the point where it killed him to do it. He would make a great throw to the plate in fielding practice, just to let the other team know that arm was there. It was an important psychological stroke. Even at the end of his career, they still weren't running on that arm.

This was the shape DiMag was in for that 1951 World Series, on October 4, when Mays finally got to see the *real* DiMaggio, his boyhood idol, in the flesh for the first time.

Willie himself did very little in that Series, getting only four hits, and all of them singles. Yet for a time it looked as though the Giants, even with Mueller's ankle keeping him on the bench and the pitching shot by the play-off, had a chance.

His first time at bat in the first inning of the opening game, Bobby Thomson was, of course, a fabulous attraction. Less than 24 hours before he had hit what the fans knew was the most famous home run of all time. Seventy thousand pairs of eyes were riveted on him. Matter of fact, the Yankees were staring at him too—so much so that while they were staring, Monte Irvin stole home.

And the Giants won the game.

They lost the second game, but won the third back at the Polo Grounds. This was the celebrated "drop kick" game in which Eddie Stanky, a sure out at second base, kicked the ball out of the glove of Yankee shortstop Phil Rizzuto and continued on to third.

"I'm not mad at him for that," said Rizzuto afterward. "What's got me sore is that he hasn't touched second base yet!"

The fans didn't notice that (remember, back in Chapter Two, it was said that this was one of the things spectators tend to overlook). But they did notice one other thing that, in this case, the experts overlooked. That was in the sixth and final game of the Series.

The Giants had a 2–1 lead in games, and would, in the

fourth game at the Polo Grounds, be opposed by Yankee right-hander Johnny Sain. Recently acquired by the Yanks from the Boston Braves, his delivery was well known to Durocher's men. That made the Giants favorites to win the fourth game.

But instead of Sain, they got rain. The game was washed out. Yankee manager Casey Stengel, given this unexpected chance to rest his pitching rotation, now could eliminate Sain from his starting plans. He did so, and the Yankees won the next three games and the Series. Their big man in that fourth game was a guy named DiMaggio, for he led them with a home run that got them tied in the Series standing, and they were never headed after that.

Wrote Mays of that final Series game:

> I'll never forget the late inning in which Stengel sent a pinch runner in for DiMaggio who was on third base. I think the fans must have realized the truth—that this was DiMag's last game of baseball. They stood and gave him a tremendous ovation as he walked to the dugout.

So here was a case where the experts didn't know—but the fans did. It was indeed Joe DiMaggio's last game.

A BASKET CASE

The return of the prodigal—Willie Mays' Fairfield homecoming after his first big league season and World Series—was something to behold. Mays himself was something to behold. He already had embarked on what over the years was to become his most enduring "hobby"— clothes.

Today, when the Giants travel, each takes a suitcase. Mays will take two suitcases, sometimes three. There is a sound reason for this, and it is not that he changes outfits much more often than his teammates or that he likes to show off.

The reason is that Willie does spend a lot for clothes— no more, though, relatively speaking, than a record collector spends on records or a stamp collector spends on stamps. Too often we regard another person's hobby as a needless luxury, forgetting our own.

And Mays feels that in many places on the road, the same-day laundry and cleaning services that ballplayers have to depend on are unnecessarily harsh on clothes. Not only that, but the risk of loss is proportionately higher. So he carries extra clothes to have enough to wear on a road trip without relying on transient cleaning facilities.

Back home in Alabama, anyway, Willie had a date with, of all people, his draft board. Writing in *Born to Play Ball*, he was philosophical about it:

> For a time, it looked like I wouldn't be going in the Army. There was a question of an aptitude test, which I had to re-take, and then the question of dependents. By now, I was contributing regularly to the support of my father, my Aunt Sarah, and my half brothers and sisters. When it was all over, though, I was scheduled for induction anyway. I was glad I'd be going in at the age of 21. That meant I'd be drafted young, instead of, say, in the middle of a baseball career. Other fellows didn't have it so lucky.

The Giants weren't having it lucky, that was for sure. They were about to lose Willie (actually, he wasn't drafted till May 29, 1952). And in a '52 spring exhibition game at Denver they did lose Monte Irvin. Going from first to third on a Mays single, Irvin slid and broke his ankle.

Willie Mays cried when he reached Irvin's side. Monte was his friend, roommate and teacher. Being married,

Irvin lived at home in New York—in 1951 and '52, Mays roomed with some Alabama friends in a seven-room railroad flat near the Polo Grounds. But on the road, he and Irvin were inseparable. Mays even bought himself a Pontiac. Why? "Cause that's what Irvin drives," he explained.

With Mays and Irvin both gone, the Giants' pennant chances in 1952 were fetched a savage blow. Mays got into 34 games at the beginning of the season, and Irvin came back late in the campaign, but for the most part the ball club was without either.

In those 34 games before he left for the Army, Mays was hitting only .236. Yet the Giants had won 27 of their first 34 games and were in first place.

It was now that the mythical Willie Mays was born.

The myth was simple:

With Mays, you win. Without him, you lose.

In 1951, with Mays the Giants won. In 1952, so long as he was with them, they won. When he left, they lost. In 1953, they lost. He came back in 1954 and they won.

It was not until 1955—when, even with Mays hitting 51 home runs, the Giants still managed to lose the pennant—that the myth was destroyed.

But by then another myth was beginning to take its place. And that was that if Mays was not in the lineup on a given day, the Giants could not win that game.

The Giants' present manager, Alvin Dark, puts stock in this visionary idea. He even had Mays start the last game of the 1961 season—a meaningless second game of a double header—so the legend could be preserved (if the Giants happened to win, Mays' name would be in the box score).

Dark needed no convincing. He had seen it for himself.

Writers who have covered the Giants ever since they
moved to San Francisco cannot remember a game the
team won when Mays' name did not appear in the box
score.

Under Dark, it did not happen very often. Though he
would rest Willie for the major parts of a few games, there
were only four times in Dark's first two years as Giant
manager that Mays failed to appear in a game at all. All
four times, Willie was hurt.

All four, incidentally, were vitally important games.
And all four, the Giants lost.

This modern extension of the myth is interesting, because Dark, remember, played on those Giant teams of
1951–'52–'53–'54. He knew Willie from 'way back.

What was interesting was that the Giants sensed the
mythical touch as early as they did. In effect, as we have
seen, they acknowledged it even before Mays became a
Giant, in the way they apologized to the Minneapolis fans
for taking him away.

Sure, he could field. But, at the time he went into the
Army, he still was unsure, sometimes throwing to a wrong
base, sometimes chasing someone else's fly ball, sometimes
(not often) doing the opposite and letting one fall in.
Shortstop Dark used to have to position him with his glove
for various hitters.

He could run, yes, but he was far from a knowing baserunner. The older and slower Dark was a far better man, ,
to select one comparison, for knowing how and when to
go on the bases.

And as for hitting, the jury was still out.

Here is Willie Mays' hitting record for his pre-Army
career with the Giants—121 games in 1951, 34 in 1952:

G	AB	H	2B	3B	HR	RBI	B.A.
155	591	157	24	9	24	91	.266

There actually were doubts, shared by Willie's greatest admirers (Leo Durocher, for one), that he would ever hit for average.

Willie's first post-Army season, 1954, was, of course, to resolve those doubts. Since the figures on games and times at bat are so close, let us state them here and now. It makes for quite a comparison. This was Willie in 1954—contrast these figures with those for 1951–52 listed just above:

G	AB	H	2B	3B	HR	RBI	B.A.
151	565	195	33	13	41	110	.345

And nobody, truthfully, expected that!

What, then, was it? We keep asking the question. We keep moving toward an answer. Spark—inspiration—quicksilver?

Maybe it was that silly cap of his (the one he was always running out from under, and still does). Once, while running full tilt for a long fly, he felt the cap start to go and put his hand up to snatch it back into place on his head. On the bench after the inning, manager Durocher said, "Willie, as a personal favor to me, will you please catch the ball first and then go get the hat?"

Mays grinned and shrugged. Afterward, he said to Alvin Dark, "Who told Leo to tell me that? You?"

"No," Dark said. "His doctor. Sudden shocks are bad for him."

The Giants were always "on" Willie. Once, in 1951, teammate Earl Rapp said to him, as they headed toward the locker room after batting practice before a game, "Race you to the clubhouse for five dollars."

"Sure," Mays said, and the two of them took off. Mays won the race by 15 yards.

"Let's have the five," he said to Rapp.

"What?" Rapp said.

"You owe me five," Willie said.

"You're crazy," Rapp said. "You owe *me* five."

"But I beat you."

"Who said anything about that? I didn't say I'd beat you for five dollars. I said I'd *race* you for five dollars. I did. Pay up."

Maybe—well, maybe it was that "Say, hey" business. Everybody called Willie "Say Hey." He was "The Say Hey Kid." Actually, that was overdrawn, though. Meeting a lot of people for the first time, and not having too good a memory for names—a lot of us share that trouble—Mays would say, by way of greeting, "Say, hey!" And the line caught on.

(Incidentally, Willie's current manager, Alvin Dark, has that same trouble with names and faces. One of the funny lines of the 1961 season, repeated in dugouts throughout the National League, was the way Alvin greeted a one-armed fan in St. Louis when the Giants played there one night. After leaving the Giants, Dark had gone on to play for the Cardinals, Cubs, Phillies, and Braves—all this before returning as the Giant manager in '61. So he had a host of fans throughout the league, and he liked to believe he remembered all of them. Anyway, in St. Louis, this one-armed fan, his right sleeve hanging empty at his side, waved cheerily at Alvin. Dark waved cheerily back at him. "Hi, Lefty!" he cried.)

But as we talk about Mays now, we are still after that elusive something—the quicksilver—and perhaps, before this story is through, we may find out what it is.

That day in May, 1952, that Willie left for the Army, manager Durocher could only say to him, "Don't get hurt."

That sounds like almost ludicrous advice for somebody who is off to be a soldier, but Leo well knew that the Army brass at whatever camp Willie went to would want him on the company teams there.

"Don't play basketball. Don't play football. If you play baseball, don't slide," Leo chanted. "I don't want you coming back to me a basket case."

Willie laughed. Perhaps he was thinking of what Leo's doctor had said.

The funny thing was that, in a manner of speaking, he *did* come back a "basket case."

In a way no one suspected.

"WILLIE WOULD'VE HAD IT"

Neither Leo nor his doctor added any years to their lives while Willie Mays was in the Army.

Mays was assigned to Camp Eustis, Virginia, where he served his draft hitch in 1952 and 1953, and sure enough, the brass had him playing baseball. Technically, he was assigned to the instructional division of the physical training department, which is Army talk for saying the Eustis brass wanted Willie on their side when the camp teams played each other.

It was an easy war for Willie. But the decision that made it an easy war was not his. If he had been sent to

Korea, he would have gone to Korea. Other baseball greats
—Jerry Coleman, Ted Williams—did go to Korea, and did
perform in combat with distinction.

But those were reserves, men who already had acquired
military specialties. Mays had none. And, like Mays, they
had no control over their orders. The fact is that, support-
ing as large a family as he did, Mays, had he been a
less prominent figure, probably would never have been
drafted at all, for men with far fewer dependents and far
less fame were winning deferments left and right in
those days. But one set of Army brass was fearful it would
look like Mays was a "special case" had he been deferred.
So he was drafted. Now another set of Army brass decided
it wanted a winning team in intercamp competition. So to
Eustis Mays went, and at Eustis he stayed.

He played basketball. When Leo Durocher heard that,
he shivered slightly.

He played baseball. At one point he fractured an ankle,
though not badly, in a slide play. Leo shivered more than
slightly.

Finally, word reached Durocher that Mays had stolen a
base with his team leading 14–0. Leo reached for the
phone. What he said to Mays on that occasion was direct,
to the point, and, in retrospect, quite funny, though it
didn't sound funny at the time. Durocher was, in effect,
seeking to operate the U. S. Army. In one small direction,
anyway.

Mays got to play in some 180 baseball games with the
Eustis team that had some other good men—Vern Law,
the Pittsburgh pitcher, and Karl Olson, the Red Sox outfielder, among them. Playing against them on another

Army team was a fair left-handed pitcher named John
Antonelli.

And while he was away, Mays learned that his Giant
teammates—some of them—had taken to paying him the
supreme compliment.

Those "some of them" were the Giant pitchers. During
1952 and 1953, while Mays was gone, Giant teams managed to lose 139 games. And when you lose, it's customarily
base hits that beat you. Base hits customarily go to the
outfield.

And so it came to pass that no matter what kind of
screaming shot left the bat and headed for the long grass,
Giant pitchers would be waiting for panting outfielders as
they came to the bench following the inning. And to each
sweatful outfielder, the pitchers would say one thing:

"Willie would've had it."

Some of those shots, he would've. Others would be
routine, of course, but a new thing was happening to
Mays. He was perfecting a way of making routine catches
look other than routine. Not that he was making the easy
catch look hard—it was just the *way* he caught the ball.

Willie had run across the "basket catch."

This was to become his trademark, a fillip far more
recognized and awaited than any such other chancy label,
like his cap flying off. It was also to become the despair of
Little League coaches from one end of the country to the
other, as their youthful players started imitating Mays and
trying to catch fly balls with their hands cupped vest-
pocket style, stomach-high, in front of them.

It is not a catch that should be imitated—Mays himself
is the first to proclaim this. In his autobiography, he
says why he adopted this fielding style:

One of the big things with me is getting the ball back to the infield as fast as possible once I make a catch. Most outfielders make their throws from the back-of-the-ear throwing position. Most of my throws, though, are made from lower down and farther out from the body, tending toward the sidearm. It occurred to me I could save a fraction of time by catching the ball lower down, too.

In the hands of a matchless technician like Mays, this might well be true. It also is true that he wears his glove farther off his hand than most outfielders, controlling it with fingertip strength. In this latter respect he established something of a trend among professional outfielders who, once they learned to control ground balls with an essentially "flapping" glove, appreciated the added inches of extra reach this grip could give them. So, at least to a modified extent, Mays has his copyists in this field.

As for catching a fly ball, though, other outfielders—some of them, like Roberto Clemente or Curt Flood, brilliant at fielding the ball in the air—still use the standard hands-up, palms-out, head-high method.

One wonders whether, perhaps subconsciously, Mays actually had another motive for developing the basket catch. That motive might be described as an instinct for showmanship. There is an element of danger in catching a fly ball the way Willie does it, for the ball is caught, essentially, without looking—without the glove in the line of sight. Mays will be looking at the ball, but his glove, down at his waist, won't.

So every fly ball becomes a challenge. Those who have watched him game in, game out over the years, still pick up a sense of risk, of derring-do, when Willie camps under a fly.

Has he ever actually dropped one? Actually, over the years he's dropped two, though in one case he was blinded by the sun. Lined up against the number of put-outs he's made since 1954, when he brought his new basket catch from the Army to the majors, this is a risk factor of approximately .0008. Over the years, in other words, Mays has drawn only two errors for failing to catch routine fly balls, and one of those was excusable.

"Is it a flair?" Leo Durocher was asked at one point.

"Call it what you want," Durocher replied.

"Did you ever ask him to change back to normal style?"

"Why should I? He catches them, doesn't he?"

And indeed he does. Furthermore, to say that he might have had a subconscious showman's reason for affecting this fielding style is not to depreciate his own reason. It may well be he *can* get the ball back faster this way. By common consent, nobody in baseball gets it back any faster.

The important thing to remember, though, is that Mays' flair, his sense of showmanship, had, and still has, two uncommon and vital ingredients:

One—As opposed to being a show-off, being a showman is quite something else again. A showman may show off, but a show-off does not necessarily have showmanship. Now, this is more than just an exercise in words. A Mays dancing off second base, drawing throw after throw from the pitcher, may strike some fans as being nothing but a show-off. The fact is, the tactic is designed basically to do one thing: help the Giants by rattling the pitcher and pulling the defense out of position. It has won games time and again.

Furthermore, Willie by nature warms to attention and notice. The very things he does to attract attention breed further exploits on his part. Mays is an actor. The ball park is his stage. But to be an actor and to have a stage is not enough. There must be an audience too.

Two—The visible ingredients of Willie's showmanship —things like the basket catch, the trick of running while looking over his shoulder, the dance step off second base —all these things are no more than ingredients. He acquired them as he went along (for instance, he showed none of the tricks just mentioned when he first came up to the Giants from Minneapolis).

But he was a showman from the very start!

And *a great ballplayer* from the very start!

Why else would the pitchers be saying, "Willie would've had it"?

Why else would a man with a .266 batting average and, as slugging outfielders go, hardly better than average power—this off his 1951–52 record—be hailed in advance as the man whose bat would drive the Giants to the 1954 pennant?

In Phoenix, where the Giants now were training, the late Jim Cruisenberry recalls a motor trip up to Las Vegas, where, in January of '54, he talked baseball with a gambling man. The Giants had finished fifth in '53, 35 games off the pace. The pennant-winning Dodgers of '53 were now the favorites to repeat. But this gambling man wasn't so sure.

"We'll tell you what the odds are," he said to Cruisenberry, "if you can tell us for sure when Mays gets out of the Army."

Cruisenberry said he wasn't sure, but he thought it would be some time in March.

"In that case," the Las Vegas man said slowly, "I'm not so sure I like the Dodgers."

CHAPTER SIXTEEN

LEO'S KIND OF TEAM

The 1954 Giants were Leo's kind of team. They were scrappers, in-fighters, hard-bitten professionals who snarled at the umpires and the opposition—and sometimes at each other—but they were a lot more than that. They were, for that one season, probably the finest major league baseball club of our time, dating back to the 1939 Yankees, who were the last of Joe McCarthy's great teams.

Sure, they had Willie Mays.

But they also had pitching—John Antonelli, the bonus baby from Rochester, New York, was with them now, along with Maglie, Hearn, Don Liddle and Ruben Gomez. In the bull pen was not one great relief pitcher but three— Hoyt Wilhelm, Marv Grissom, and Windy McCall. That meant Durocher could, and did, go to his bench for the pinch hitter as early as the fourth and fifth innings, not because his starting pitcher was going bad but because he could afford to go for power right away, knowing the bull pen would hold the lead.

Here is the story of that pitching, expressed in statistical form. They say statistics don't lie. Sometimes they're wrong when they say that. But this time they're right. These statistics *don't* lie:

The Giants won 97 games in 1954.

In 60 of those 97, the other team was held to two runs or under!

In all of '54, there were only four games where the other team was held to two runs or fewer and still beat the Giants.

In those low-run games, therefore, the Giants were winners 60 out of 64 times—a winning factor of exactly 94 percent!

All right. So much for the pitching. Now, how about the power? That bench power that good pitching made possible to use to its fullest extent delivered as no bench in history ever delivered before.

The Giants had ten pinch-hit home runs in 1954.

Nine of them won ball games!

But there was more to it than that—three singles, for example, delivered by that same bench—as we shall see.

Fine, then—we have pitching and bench power.

Well, then, how about defense?

The defense was there. It was good. It was important, so important that a .188 hitter, catcher Wes Westrum, worked as the regular, he was that good at handling pitchers, pop fouls, steals, and tag plays.

Westrum, of course, was the first man in the familiar defensive axis that makes or breaks a ball club. "Down the middle," they call it. It starts with your catcher. It includes your second baseman—now it was Davey Williams, replacing the scrappy Stanky and in some respects, including range and speed, Stanky's superior. It includes your shortstop—now it was Alvin Dark at the peak of his career.

And it casts its anchor in center field.

And there was Willie Mays.

Frank Forbes, a Giant scout who had been retained as a personal contact with Mays (among other things), was at the gates of Camp Eustis the day Willie got out of the Army.

It was a cold, blustery day in March. Mays and Forbes drove to the Washington, D. C., airport, and in the chilling temperatures Forbes, with no intention of delivering a chilled Willie to Leo Durocher in Phoenix, wrapped his own overcoat around Mays, even adding a lining of newspaper to the insides. To airport police, this made an interesting sight—particularly because, earlier that day, a quartet of deranged Puerto Rican revolutionists had shot up the House of Representatives, wounding five congressmen.

There was time out for rapid identification. To this day, a couple of Washington policemen think of a bulky, furtive-looking subversive every time they hear of Willie Mays.

When he got to Phoenix, the Giants acted as if they didn't know him, either.

"Who *is* that?" Whitey Lockman kept asking, scratching his head.

"Face is kind of familiar," Sal Maglie said.

Willie puts a "World Series effort" into a leap to catch a fly during training at the New York Giants camp in Phoenix, Arizona, in 1956.

"Looks like a rookie we had with us for a while in '52," Alvin Dark said. "Lasted twenty-seven games, I think it was. You know rookies. Here today, gone tomorrow. Couldn't hit the curve ball."

"That's right," Monte Irvin said. "That's who it is. Hey, kid, what'd you say your name was?"

"Hey," Mays piped. "What's that matter with all of you?"

"We're just trying to place you," Dark said.

"*Place* me!" Mays said. "How long I got to put up with this stuff, Leo?"

"That's enough, men," Durocher said. He turned to Mays. "How many games *did* you play in '52?"

"Twenty-seven."

"Sounds like Alvin's right, then," Leo said. "Never mind, though, son. We'll give you a try. Let's see you swing the bat." To the batting practice pitcher at Phoenix Municipal Stadium, Durocher called "Throw him a curve!"

"A *curve?*" Mays cried. "Man, nobody hit a curve this early in the year."

"Sounds like Alvin's right, then," Durocher said again. "Doesn't want to hit the curve ball."

"That's who it is, all right," Dark said. "That same rookie we had in '52. Flashy, but no staying power."

"Gimme a bat," Mays said, and went and stood in the batting cage. "Curve ball!" he yelled at the pitcher.

Behind him, Durocher made a motion with his hand. On the mound, the pitcher grinned, wound up and threw —not a curve but a fast ball.

Trapped, Mays swung savagely.

The ball was still going up when it left the ball park. It cleared the light tower in left field, the palm trees beyond.

In the stands, Horace Stoneham, chatting with scouts Tom Sheehan and Carl Hubbell, jumped to his feet. "Did you see that?" he cried. "Did you *see* it?"

"How could you see it?" Hubbell said. "He hit it downtown."

"Downtown is right," Sheehan said. "Downtown Denver."

On the field, Mays came back to the bench. He surveyed the players sitting there. "Okay," he said. "Now do you remember who I am?"

Leo Durocher shrugged. "We still don't know if you can hit a curve."

"Oh, what do you got to do around here?" Mays moaned. "What do you got to do?"

Up in the press box, sports writer Barney Kremenko was looking at the scene on the field. Willie Mays was back. Something had happened. Not to Mays, though. To the rest of the ball club.

"You know something," Kremenko said, "I've got a feeling this center fielder is underpaid."

Mays had signed for $13,000 in 1954.

He himself didn't think he was underpaid. At one point, another writer asked him if he was going to ask for $25,000, and Mays' eyes bugged wide. "They shoot me, I ask for that kind of money," he said.

Mr. Kremenko, it turned out, was correct.

THE NEW BABE RUTH

Leo's kind of team, those 1954 Giants were.

In a game against the Dodgers, Maglie and the Giants led 2–1 with two out in the ninth and two strikes on Roy Campanella, only to see Campy tie it with a home run. It went that way, 2–2, till the top of the 13th, when Don Hoak homered for Brooklyn.

Now it was the last of the 13th, and with two out the Giants loaded the bases on three walks. By this time, catcher Westrum had been replaced by Ray Katt. Now, Durocher called on Dusty Rhodes to pinch-hit for Katt.

As Rhodes went to select a bat, Durocher said to him, "Any questions?"

"Yes," Dusty said. "Who's going to catch the 14th if we tie it?"

"You are," Durocher snapped.

"Me? I can't catch."

"Then there better not be any 14th inning," Leo said.

Rhodes went up to the plate and singled. In came Mueller from third with the tying run. Here came Mays, being waved around third by coach Herman Franks.

And Rhodes, as he legged out his hit, found himself yelling, "Run, Willie! For my sake!"

Willie slid in ahead of the throw and the Giants had won it, 4–3.

That was one of the pinch singles mentioned in the last chapter—singles that went overlooked in retrospect, when people marveled over the glamour of all those pinch-hit home runs.

Another time, Monte Irvin beat the Braves with a pinch single. Irvin had been hitless his previous 26 times at bat.

Another time, Durocher had Rhodes pinch-hit for Irvin —a move so unexpected (for Irvin was going well at the time) that it left the visiting Brooklyn club helpless to counteract the percentage move by bringing in a left-hander to pitch to Rhodes. They simply had no left-hander warmed up. So Rhodes singled for two runs and the Giants won.

A gambling man, Durocher, and he held the hot hand. In another game against the Dodgers, he had his pitcher intentionally walk Brooklyn's eighth-place hitter to *force* the Dodgers to pinch-hit for *their* pitcher—which the Dodgers obediently did. The Giants got rid of the pinch hitter on a fly ball, and went on to win the game. Leo had had a hunch they'd score better off Brooklyn's relief pitcher than off the starter. So he got the Dodgers to change their pitcher for him!

Meanwhile, out in center field . . .

Well, on opening day (and it was Giants vs. Dodgers again, at the Polo Grounds) the score was 3–3 in the last of the sixth, and Willie Mays now hit a home run into Section 35—upstairs in deep left field—to win it, 4–3.

At Ebbets Field, first time the Giants played there in '54, Mays homered again. At Wrigley Field, Chicago, on April 30, he homered in the 14th inning. At County Stadium, Milwaukee, he homered. Against the Phillies on May 24, Mays homered twice. The Giants beat the Pirates 21 to 4 (Mays homered) and then 2 to 1 (Mays homered). Against the Dodgers, Mays homered. At St. Louis, on June 3, Mays homered twice. He homered against the Cubs. Against the Cards on June 21, he homered twice. This was the start of a stretch in which he was to hit six home runs in five games—and in all five of those games, he homered on his first time at bat.

The last of that home-run streak came against the Cubs at the Polo Grounds. It was an inside-the-park job, on a hot night, and the exertion of it brought a wave of dizziness over Mays when he went out to take his position in center field.

It had happened to him once before—in that sandlot game back home in Alabama, years earlier.

It would happen to him once again, years later, in 1962, again on a hot night. And that time—well, we'll get to that time when we get to it.

But at this time, in 1954, these things were happening:

Giant fans scheduled a "day" for Mays at the Polo Grounds—an unprecedented salute to a twenty-three-year-old who had, up to that time, played little more than a hundred games before the home fans.

Time Magazine put Mays on its cover.

Frank Forbes said to him, "You've finally become a celebrity—one of the gossip columnists says you're about to be married."

Two songs were written about him.

He was hailed as—of all things—a stickball player.

Now, stickball is a game played on the sidewalks (or, more accurately, in the streets) of New York City. Distances are measured by sewers (manhole covers), the ball is a rubber ball or a handball, the pitcher throws on one bounce, the hitter uses a broomstick for a bat, first base and third base are the fenders of parked cars, second and home are sewers. Summer nights in New York, when it stayed light till after 8 o'clock, Mays would descend to St. Nicholas Place from his room in the five-room apartment of a housemotherly type named Mrs. David Goosby, whom the Giants had placed in charge of their prize.

And, with the neighborhood kids for teammates and opponents, Willie would play stickball.

"I can almost always pick up a game with some of the kids on the block," he explained, by way of what may go down in history as the most remarkable understatement of the twentieth century.

Some of the kids on the block suspected Willie of wanting to take batting practice.

"Seems like he's always up," one of them said dolefully.

"I threw him my Sunday pitch," one of the pitchers said. "I said, 'Hit that one!' He did. For three sewers. My outfielder didn't even chase the ball. My outfielder say to me, 'What do you expect? It's *him.*'"

(A fine professional ballplayer of nearly a decade later, third baseman Cletis Boyer of the New York Yankees, was to utter the same thought, and close to the same words, after a game in the 1962 World Series. Boyer had lined a wicked liner to right center. "As I started to run," he recounted later, "my mind was telling me, That's a double—maybe a triple. Then all of a sudden I remembered. I said to myself, *He's* out there." Mays was out there, indeed, cutting the ball off in midair to turn a sure hit into what, for him, was a more-or-less routine put-out. So accepted are Mays' fielding skills that none of the papers next day bothered to point out that with anyone else, as Boyer himself had observed bitterly, this would have been at least a double.)

Mays in 1954 was described by Gilbert Milstein, an acute writer for *The New York Times,* as Rousseau's natural man. George Jessel, the comedian, said, "It's possible at this rate that even Willie Mays will be forgotten in two thousand years." Jessel said this upon learning that a great many Italians never heard of Julius Caesar. One of the most knowing sources, a shortstop in the Negro National League named Jack Hardy who had seen Mays over the years, described him in one word: "Unbelievable." Leo Durocher said, simply and point-blank, that Mays was "the greatest player I ever laid eyes on."

Incidentally, this greatest player didn't make the starting berth in center field for the National League All-Stars that year! Duke Snider of Brooklyn, himself having his best season, beat Willie out. (But this kind of thing bothers the fans more than anybody else. It had happened before, would happen again. As recently as 1961, the great Frank Robinson of Cincinnati, en route to leading the

Reds to the pennant and becoming the league's most valuable player, couldn't break into the NL's starting All-Star lineup.)

Indeed, to Mays was paid the tribute supreme: that he looked good striking out. This had been said of only one player in baseball history: Babe Ruth.

And thereby hung the Mays story in 1954.

He was running ahead—well ahead—of Babe Ruth's record home run pace—the one that brought the Babe his 60 homers in 1927.

On July 28, Mays hit his 36th home run (24 of those 36 had come against right-handed pitchers, supposedly Willie's nemesis).

But the Giants had been losing some ball games. What's that? This greatest modern-day team losing? Yes, indeed. Nor is the explanation hard to come by. Durocher's men were in the process of making up a 35-game trailing margin from the year before—against essentially the same competition that had created that 35-game gap. This in fact was the Giants' first sign of greatness, for ever since mid-June they had led the league.

But on July 29, they lost to the Cardinals 8–0, and a storm broke loose in the New York papers. Manager Durocher had pulled Lockman out of the game, and Lockman had thrown a couple of towels.

As we said before of this Giant club of '54, they fought—sometimes with each other.

The papers said it was dissension—the Giants were through—they had fallen apart.

It had started, though no one noticed the significance at the time, on a road trip where a grieving Mays, jolted by news that his beloved Aunt Sarah had died, left the team to attend the funeral in Fairfield.

He rejoined the club in Milwaukee. There was a taxicab race from the airport to the ball park. Mays was in the clubhouse, getting dressed, when his former teammate, Bobby Thomson, hit the pinch single that was to beat the Giants 3–2 in the ninth.

This was the mild beginning of the new myth—the one that has grown ever since—that without Willie in the lineup, the Giants could not win.

But with him in the lineup, they still weren't winning.

The lead was down to three games over Brooklyn (it had been 6½); then two; then one.

A flareup or two in the clubhouse. Lockman's momentary but public display on the field. . . .

And in the locker room after that, Leo Durocher quietly called one of his players into his private office.

That player was Willie Mays.

"Willie," Durocher said to him, "I want to ask you to do something to help the team."

"Sure, Skip," Mays said. "What is it?"

"Quit hitting home runs!"

CHAPTER
EIGHTEEN

"WE'RE CELEBRATING
EARLY"

It sounded unbelievable.

But Leo meant every word he said.

And, to a baseball man, it meant sense.

Expressed at its most basic, it came down to two inter-weaving concepts:

Mays, going for the long ball, was not being used to his optimum potential—which was, of course, as a baserunner

Mays, going for the long ball, was having long flies caught on him—the balls that almost got out of the park but didn't.

Something had happened—even the fans grew to sense it, though they guessed the wrong reason. The man with 36 home runs in late July now hit only five more homers

116

the rest of the way—and of those five, two were inside-the-park jobs, another two came after the pennant was assured.

Most people guessed Mays was under instructions to "meet" the ball because he had been striking out too much. But he was hitting .320 at the time Durocher called off the homers. He couldn't have been striking out *that* much!

What Durocher did do, instead of a specific instruction to "meet" the ball, was to suggest to Mays that he start going for right field—punching the ball, in other words, in fealty to what Wee Willie Keeler said years and years before: "Hit 'em where they ain't." A Mays who would hit to right field would spread-eagle the defense, making it impossible for them to bunch on his power.

At the same time, Durocher moved Mays from sixth to fourth in the batting order, meaning big hitters would be coming up behind him. Moving Willie forward in the order also increased his chances of getting an extra time at bat in the ninth inning of a game.

So, here is what happened:

Mays promptly went on a 21-game hitting streak.

The Giants launched a six-game winning streak, fell back, then went to work on a new seven-game winning streak.

The high point of that winning streak was a double-header sweep of the Pirates, by scores of 5 to 4 and 5 to 3, in which Mays never once even got the ball out of the infield. That was the day his hitting streak came to an end.

But by then, the Giants were home free.

Early in September, they opened a three-game series with the second-place Dodgers at the Polo Grounds. The first game was a wild one, and Leo wanted it—wanted it bad. The Giants led the Dodgers by three games in the standings. A win tonight should do it.

With the score tied at 4–4 (thanks to a pinch-hit single by Irvin that scored two runs in the bottom of the sixth), the Giants had two out in the last of the seventh with Mueller on third and Davey Williams on first.

Relief pitcher Hoyt Wilhelm was due to bat.

Leo had one of his hunches.

He decided to let Wilhelm hit for himself.

This was something that just wasn't done. Wilhelm had been allowed to hit for himself only 15 times all year—and was out all 15 times.

If 46,611 fans were bewildered, you should have seen the Dodgers.

On the one hand, they had to look out for the double steal. On the other, they had to figure out how to pitch to Wilhelm. None of them had ever seen him bat!

So—Wilhelm singled to center to beat them, and that night there were suspicious sounds of revelry from the Giant clubhouse.

It was only September 3.

But, said a clubhouse boy, "I guess you could say we're celebrating early!"

Which they had every right to do. They had a lock on the pennant, and rightfully enough it was another Dodger game, the final Monday of the season, that clinched the flag mathematically for the Giants.

Durocher had thought of resting some of his main players the rest of the way, using them just enough to keep them from going stale, but now Mueller and Mays were hooked up with Duke Snider of Brooklyn in a three-way race for the batting title.

Going to right field may have cost Mays some home runs, but it was to put 25 late-season points on his batting average.

The morning of the final Sunday of the season, the individual hitting race looked like this:

	AB	H	B.A.
Mueller	613	210	.3426
Snider	581	199	.3425
Mays	561	192	.3422

Percentage-wise, Mueller and Snider had the edge that last day, since both were left-handed hitters going against right-handed pitchers, Mueller against Robin Roberts of Philadelphia and Snider against Jake Thies of Pittsburgh, while Mays, a right-handed batsman, would be swinging (opposed by Roberts) *against* the percentage.

But in their final times at bat, Snider went hitless in three trips; Mueller got two hits in six trips; Mays got three in four!

The final standing read, as a result:

	AB	H	B.A.
Mays	565	195	.345
Mueller	619	212	.343
Snider	584	199	.341

That night on television, Ed Sullivan asked Mays what it felt like to beat out his own teammate for the batting crown.

Willie blinked. Think like a diplomat for a minute here—what would *you* have said?

Finally, Mays said, "Well, it was good to know that if it hadn't been me it would've been him."

Not a bad line for a ballplayer—or a diplomat.

Next day, though, Mays was a trifle less diplomatic.

He'd had two television appearances the night before, and one this morning. Now he had to go to the Polo Grounds for a round of picture-taking. Autograph hounds, reporters, ticket-seekers, surrounded him in a clamoring, never-ending mass.

Right fielder Mueller, of course, was understandably disappointed at leading the league in total hits and still seeing himself edged out of the batting title on the final day of the season. Not the world's greatest fielder, he was nonetheless more than adequate at his position—but here too he was overshadowed.

So, for separate reasons, neither he nor Mays were at their genial best as they dressed in the clubhouse that Monday.

Willie was tying a shoe as Mueller walked by him.

"Is it true," Mueller said to him faintly, "what I've been reading in the papers? That you're the best center fielder in history?"

Mays looked up. "Best right fielder too," he said.

That was all. He went back to tying his shoe.

This was supposed to be the guy whose vocabulary was limited to "Say, hey."

THE CATCH

They gave the 1954 Giants a ticker tape parade—
something no other New York team ever received. The
place of honor in the first open car in the procession that
worked its way up lower Broadway went to Alvin Dark
and Willie Mays. "Don't give me any credit," Leo
Durocher told the huge crowd at City Hall. "I didn't pitch
a ball or hit one all season long."

It was a parade that came after the Giants won the
pennant, but before the start of the World Series. Better
salute them while they were winning—they sure weren't
going to win the World Series.

Officially, the Cleveland Indians were 8 to 5 favorites.

Among friends it was 2 to 1. In some American League towns it was as much as 13 to 5.

And why not? Hadn't they won an all-time-record 111 games in their league?

But, well, there were some things people didn't take into consideration, like:

Two teams, the Yankees and White Sox, were the only others in the American League to have played better-than-.500 ball that season. And on the season, despite those 111 triumphs, the best the Indians could do against the good competition was break even. What they had done was simply to mop up against the weak sisters. Even the schedule favored them, for the competition—the Yanks and Sox—were in different geographical divisions, East and West, which meant the Indians never had to play them in consecutive, uninterrupted series.

The Giants, by contrast, had six tough teams in their league (the sixth-place St. Louis Cardinals in the National won more games than the fourth-place Boston Red Sox in the American). Six tough teams, and the other two could beat you (last-place Pittsburgh, winner of only 53 games all year, beat the Dodgers four straight in September). Yet the Giants won their season's series from each of the seven other teams in the league.

The Indians were famous for their pitching, headed by Bob Lemon, Mike Garcia, Early Wynn—20-game-winners all. But, as we have already noted, the Giant pitching wasn't exactly bad. They'd tossed 19 shut-outs, 22 one-run games, 23 two-run games.

Perhaps most important of all, and most overlooked, was the annual spring-training series of games between the two teams in Arizona. The Giants had mopped up. People forgot that.

The first game, at the Polo Grounds, was a 2 2 game going into the top of the eighth. Then Larry Doby led off for Cleveland with a walk and Al Rosen followed with an infield hit.

At bat now was Vic Wertz, who so far, against Giant starter Sal Maglie, had tripled in the first, singled in the fourth, singled again in the sixth.

Durocher replaced Maglie with Don Liddle, but nobody was doing anything to control Wertz this day. Liddle threw, Wertz swung, and there it went, on a rising, soaring line toward deepest center field, just to the right of dead center.

Possessed of the instinct that only he, Joe DiMaggio, and a handful of others have exhibited, Mays literally was underway *before* the ball was hit. Knowing what the pitch was, seeing the bat come around, he sensed what would happen now. The result was that as those behind home plate looked up to follow the flight of Wertz' hit, all they saw was that famous number—*24*. Willie's back was already turned full to the diamond.

It was to be by no means his greatest catch, even though, to this day, it is referred to as The Catch. He had running room—the Polo Grounds' center field was the deepest in either major league. The ball "stayed up," as he put it— was in the air long enough for Mays, who played then (and still plays) a relatively short center field (the shortest, it has been said, since Speaker), to make his deep run.

Just this side of the 460-foot sign at the base of the bleachers, Mays caught the ball, over his left shoulder, going away, like an end being "led" by a long-passing quarterback in football.

Because it came at the moment it did—in the opening game of a World Series, with, as they say, "the game on the bases" at the time—this was to become a famous play.

Even more so, because it broke the Indians' collective back.

But what was fantastic about it was what happened now.

Somehow, in full all-out stride away from the infield, Mays turned, wheeled, and powered the ball back to Davey Williams at second. Doby, tagged up at second, did make it to third. Rosen had to scamper like crazy to *get back* to first.

The Giants got out of the inning.

And the game went on.

It went into the top of the tenth, and here Mr. Wertz was up again. And here he went, this time with a vicious, low liner to left-center (Mays was playing him in right-center). This one didn't "stay up." But somehow Willie got to it, gloved it one-handed on a tricky bounce—what was it Kitty-Kat had said, so long ago? "Picking it up is something you can never practice enough!"—and held Wertz to a double on what should have been a triple, could have been an inside-the-park homer.

And again the Giants got out of the inning.

In the bottom of the tenth, the Indians brought in a new catcher. Leading off for the Giants, Mays watched him idly, from the on-deck circle. The catcher was a veteran, Mickey Grasso. He took Lemon's warm-up throws, then fired routinely to second, and Willie noticed something.

That throw from Grasso to second base had got there on the bounce.

A little thing? Baseball is made up of little things.

Willie, leading off, drew a walk. Promptly, he lit out for second base. The throw from Grasso came, once again, on the bounce—and Mays had it stolen.

Now Cleveland manager Al Lopez had to put the force on by issuing an intentional pass to Henry Thompson. And now, with Monte Irvin due up, here came Dusty Rhodes instead—and there went a lazy fly down the right-field line and up against the facade beneath the upper stand, just past the short foul pole, for the game-winning homer!

The next day, Rhodes was to single, then homer again, as the Giants won the game. The Indians had got out in front 1–0 when their lead-off man, Al Smith, hit Antonelli's first pitch of the game for a wrong-field homer. Then, in that same top half of the first inning, Antonelli walked Al Rosen and Wertz, and Wally Westlake singled on a vicious, hopping track over second base. In center field, Mays charged the ball like an infielder, scooped it up one-handed—what was it Kitty-Kat had said, so long ago? "Picking it up is something you can never practice enough!"—and when the Cleveland third-base coach, Tony Cuccinello, saw that, he put his hands miserably up in the air, and Rosen stopped at third. By then, catcher Westrum already had the ball. It had roared in on the fly, head-high all the way, from the man in center field.

"That," said Cleveland manager Al Lopez after the Series ended, "was the key play. The key play of the whole business."

It was, too, for though nobody, not even the most rabid
Giant fan, could have guessed it, the Indians were never
to go ahead again—not even for an inning in the scoreboard—in the whole Series. They did make their 1–0 lead
stand up till the fifth—Early Wynn hadn't permitted a
Giant baserunner to that point. But leading off the fifth,
Mays worked Wynn for a walk. Instantly, Henry Thompson rifled a single to right field.

Batting for Monte Irvin? Dusty Rhodes. There went a
run-scoring single, and before the inning was out the
Giants had a second run to lead 2–1. Rhodes' subsequent
seventh-inning home run made the final score what it
was, 3–1.

Now the Giants accompanied ("dragged" might be a
better word) the Indians to Cleveland for the resumption
of the Series there.

In the first inning of the third game, Lockman singled
off Mike Garcia's opening pitch. Then the Indian shortstop made a bad throw on a double-play ball and the
Giants had a man on second with two out.

Mays singled to right field and the Giants led 1–0.

In the top of the third, the Giants had men on second
and third with one out. The Indians issued the automatic
base on balls to Thompson. So—"Attention, Ladies and
Gentlemen: Rhodes now batting for Irvin!"

And Dusty slammed Garcia's first pitch to right field for
a two-run single. Back of Ruben Gomez, the Giants won
it 6–2.

Three straight from the Indians (who somehow had had
37 runners to the Giants' 28, yet had been outscored
14 to 5).

That final game was a strange one. Fielding blunders by the Indians helped the Giants to a quick 2–0 lead (the big hit was a double by Irvin—batting for himself!). By the time the game was halfway through, the Giants were ahead 7–0.

The Indians managed to get four runs back, and then, in the last of the eighth, an uncanny thing took place.

Giant reliefer Hoyt Wilhelm, a great knuckle-baller, started things out by striking out Cleveland second baseman Bobby Avila, the American League's batting champion.

At the point where Avila swung and missed at the third strike, the ball was in the strike zone. At the point a couple of feet farther, where catcher Westrum was waiting for the ball, it was over his head for a passed ball, and Avila easily made it to first base.

That knuckle ball had jumped so crazily that the official scorers decided that they'd have to give the error not to Westrum, the catcher, but to Wilhelm, the pitcher!

With one out, Rosen now got a single, and at this point Westrum took off his mask, called time, and summoned Durocher out of the dugout for a conference.

"What's the matter?" Durocher wanted to know. "Do you want a new pitcher? Hasn't he got enough?"

Westrum began to laugh. "I want a new catcher. He's got too much!"

It was a way of saying that Wilhelm, at that moment, was *too good*.

That knuckle ball was dancing in a way no one, least of all the pitcher, could control. And with men on the bases, a pitch that got away now could be unnecessarily costly.

Despite himself, Durocher began to laugh too.

Al Dark came in from his shortstop position and joined the conversation.

Final decision: bring Antonelli in from the bull pen.

John came in, struck out Wertz and Westlake, and good night, ladies.

The Giants had swept the heavily favored Indians four straight in the World Series.

It was the only time before or since that an *underdog* ever *swept* a Series.

And they won it easily. Breezing. Going away, with a laughing conference at the pitcher's mound in the final game.

The pitching had done it, of course. Dark and Mueller had delivered seven hits apiece. Lockman was a key man. Westrum had done an unsung but heady job behind the plate. Davey Williams had been a star.

And, of course, Dusty Rhodes—the uncanny pinch-hitting hero.

Mays? Well, he'd made that catch—THE CATCH—in the first game.

He had an equal, though, in third baseman Henry Thompson, whose fielding had been superb—and who always seemed to "be there" when the Giants were scoring.

Let's digress for a minute. Suppose A gets on base on an error. B hits a single, sending him to third. C now grounds out, while A scores. What does that mean? It means that in the record book, A gets credit for a run scored, C gets credit for a run batted in. But B, the only man who got a hit in the inning, the man who made the run possible, gets no credit in the book toward run production!

So, no matter how they talked about Rhodes—and he deserved every word of praise he got—the fact remains that if you dissect the Giants' scoring innings in that World Series of 1954 into three parts—runs scored, batted in, or *advanced to scoring position*—then, of the 11 innings in which the Giants scored runs, Thompson figured in seven.

That was more than Rhodes.

Matter of fact, it was more than any other man, using the same realistic index—except one.

Totally unnoticed, one other man figured in *eight* of those 11 scoring innings.

That one other man was Willie Mays.

HUMAN AFTER ALL

Willie Mays was the National League's most valuable player, by overwhelming vote, for the 1954 season. Perhaps even more significantly, in a year in which man first ran the four-minute mile and records fell in many sports, he won the Associated Press poll as "athlete of the year."

It would be nice to say that the next year he hit more than 50 home runs.

Since it's nice to say, let's say it—he *did* hit more than 50 homers in 1955—51, to be exact, tying him with John Mize for the all-time homer high by a Giant. He had already, in '54, set the all-time mark for extra-base hits by a Giant in one season, with 87. He was now set to embark on another record-tying feat—leading the National League four consecutive years in stolen bases.

Which was interesting, because it began to seem that the older Mays got, the faster he became. That's not quite the way it was, of course. What he was doing was adding know-how to instinct. This way he would pass his thirtieth birthday and still be leading his club, year in and year out, in stolen bases.

And there was the story—know-how.

In a sense, 1954 was the last year for the "old" Willie Mays—the carefree, stickball-playing, happy-go-lucky Say Hey Kid.

Perhaps that play on Wertz—The Catch—in the 1954 Series played its part. Wherever he went afterward, people wanted to hear about The Catch. Yet his own baseball knowledge told him that it hadn't been that great a play! The one he made on Wertz two innings later, holding that wicked skimmer to a double, was a far more difficult, more brilliantly executed play. Yet it went virtually unnoticed by press and public alike.

"It ain't no play unless you catch it," Willie said, a little wistfully. Among other things, he was beginning to realize, for the first time, that the spectators don't always see the things that go on.

In Puerto Rico, where he played winter ball in between the '54 and '55 seasons, Willie got into a much-publicized scuffle with Giant teammate Ruben Gomez over whose right it was at that moment to occupy the batting cage.

In New York, the agency handling his personal appearances and testimonials discovered that Mays had okayed the use of his name by two different soft-drink companies.

Again in New York—and again, this was 1955—Mays

charged a ball hit by Duke Snider. He missed the shoe-string try, and the ball went through him. Willie didn't chase it. The fans booed him, and next day, sports writer Joe King wrote:

> Maybe success did come too fast for the young man. Maybe the dramatic Negro boy the Giants plucked out of deep South obscurity has failed to appreciate that last year was a freak and that baseball is a job you work at 60 minutes an hour, and that the prima donnas are hated worse than any other by the fans. That's what Willie was yesterday—a prima donna.

Well, maybe last year (1954) wasn't a "freak" and maybe the Giants didn't exactly pluck Mays from ob-scurity, but he sure was a prima donna on that occasion.

Another time in '55, at Milwaukee, he looked so bad on the bases, taking outrageous gambles that had no rhyme or reason, that manager Durocher sat him down for a game.

"He's confused," Leo said.

Willie has been "confused" on other occasions. He has misjudged fly balls (well, actually, he has misjudged *one* fly ball—in Milwaukee, in 1961, but as we will tell, he made up for it later). He once failed to run out a foul pop, though there was a chance the wind would blow it fair—which in fact happened. On occasion he has loafed on a hit, losing the extra base as a result, although here you begin to wonder whether such an occasional lapse is a sin or a virtue—for a "loafing" Mays can recover and turn it on with such blinding speed that the very act of loafing can, and has, suckered the defense into making a bad play.

And again here, the fans don't always see it right. Mays has purposely made himself look bad on the bases, from time to time, in order to draw a play away from a team mate. This is nothing more or less than practical baseball. If the teammate is going to be out, and Mays, the best baserunner on the team, can lure a throw against himself, he may be out instead, but he has the better chance of being safe. If one sure out is the worst that can happen, the gamble has nothing to lose.

But we were talking about things Willie's done wrong.

Well, there was the time in New York in '56 when he overslid third, the time in San Francisco in '62 when he did the same, the time he swung at intentional ball four and popped it up, the time (already mentioned in this book) when he wandered off third base, thinking three were out.

Once, he was at a boys' club function, and one of his young admirers said, "Willie, I wish I could be a ball-player like you."

"Maybe you will be," Mays said.

The youngster shook his head. "No. I make mistakes."

"I make mistakes too," Willie said.

"*You* make mistakes?"

"Sure I do."

The master of ceremonies interrupted to say, "He's human after all, aren't you, Willie?"

But Mays ignored him and went on talking to the youngster. "The thing to do," he said seriously, "is to *know* when you've done wrong. And bear down harder afterward. I saw a bunch of kids in a Pony League game one time, and the umpire made a bad call, and they yelled at him, and finally that umpire turned to them and he

said, 'Don't get so upset. It's only a game.' And it is a
game. But you still got to try the best you know how. And
you know who wasn't trying in that game? That umpire,
that's who. It was okay that he made a bad call. That'll
happen. But to act like he didn't know he'd made a mistake—that's the part you got to look out for."

Willie Mays grinned ruefully. "Do I make mistakes?
You want a simple answer? The simple answer is yes."

SLUMP

The Mays who could do no wrong was a thing of the past, no doubt about it. Yet did such a superman ever exist to begin with? Obviously not. During the Giants' pennant run in 1951, remember, he once failed to touch third while running out an inside-the-park homer; he crashed into teammate Irvin on another occasion.

The pure fact is that, as time went by, Mays (understandably enough) was making *fewer and fewer* mistakes. There had been a time, for example, when he threw to the wrong base with some measure of unhappy consistency. Not only did he cure that habit, but sometimes startled his own teammates with an uncanny sixth sense of where to throw the ball.

135

Once in 1962, for example, Henry Aaron of Milwaukee was on first base and a teammate hit a longish, slicing drive to right-center. Mays made the catch and Aaron, already around second, had to double furiously back to first. There was doubt whether he'd make it ahead of Willie's throw.

But Willie never threw to first. He rifled the ball to second instead, where shortstop Jose Pagan took the ball standing on the bag.

And Aaron was out! He'd neglected to touch second on his way back to first.

(Afterward, disbelievers asked Pagan if he'd yelled to Willie to throw the ball to second. Pagan said, simply, "No.")

"When that center fielder gets the ball," Bill Rigney, the Giants' manager from 1956 through mid-1960, would tell rookie infielders at spring training, "you go to a base. Never mind whether you think he's going to throw it there or not. Just be there in case he does. And don't ask me why."

No, the Mays who could do no wrong existed mainly in the minds of the fans—just as sometimes the Mays who did do wrong existed only in their imagination too. Perhaps a St. Louis writer expressed it best when, watching Willie in center field during a late inning in the 1954 All-Star game, he saw a shiny object on the ground not far away.

"Hey, look," the writer said. "Willie's halo just fell off."

The halo fell off, as we have noted, in 1955, simply because that was the year that, for the first time, the Giants had Willie and still couldn't win the pennant.

So that myth was dead. Cold stone dead in the market, for in some respects Mays had had an even better year than in '54—consider his 51 homers (10 more than the previous year) and his 127 runs batted in (17 more).

Then in 1956, Willie acquired what the jokers called "two new managers." Bill Rigney succeeded Durocher as Giant manager, and Willie got married.

Many pundits like to think that this is what caused his "bad" year in 1956—his slump. This business of getting used to new people and new responsibilities. The part about getting used to people is probably overstated. But the responsibilities were there.

On the field, they developed a startling new context. It began with Rigney's assigning the veteran Hank Sauer to play left field for the Giants at the Polo Grounds. Rig wanted Sauer's bat in the lineup. But Sauer, slow afoot, was a liability in the outfield—except that now Willie Mays was "shading" him, playing his own position and some of Sauer's too.

This was to be the first of the difficult years, not only for Mays but for the Giants. The club was rebuilding; there was a new manager; within two years the Giants would move to San Francisco, there to be greeted with mixed emotions by the local populace. The turnover would be something to behold, especially following that move to the Pacific Coast. Compare the Giants with the Dodgers, who moved to Los Angeles at the same time the Giants moved to San Francisco. Of the holdover Dodger stars from Brooklyn who took the field for their first game in Los Angeles, a dozen men, including the manager and the top pitcher, were still with the club three years later. Of the New York Giants who took the field for the first time in San Francisco, only one—Mays—was still around three years later.

His slump in 1956 resulted in a .296 batting average (his only time under .300) and a career low of 84 runs batted in. Does that mean Willie wasn't trying? Hardly. He led the league in stolen bases (he stole third 13 times in 13 attempts!), causing the legendary Ty Cobb to remark that Mays had singlehandedly restored the art—that's what Cobb called it, and rightfully so—of baserunning to the game. In the All-Star game, an affair which over the years has produced a plus-.400 batting average for Willie and more individual records than any other player's, he got in only as a pinch hitter—and whacked a pinch homer off Whitey Ford.

And in Pittsburgh's Forbes Field he made what those who have seen all of Mays' games with the Giants—and that select few includes broadcaster Russ Hodges—was the greatest catch they ever saw him or anybody make.

It didn't get the attention the Wertz catch got—after all, that was a World Series, this was a game between second-division clubs (the Giants finished sixth in '56, the Pirates seventh).

But, with bases loaded, Roberto Clemente hit one to the light tower in left center-field, and Willie Mays went and got it. Just to say it doesn't describe it.

"Mays makes a lot of great catches that nobody notices," sportscaster Hodges has said, "because he gets there before the ball does. Nobody sees the jump he got on the ball that enabled him to get there. But in this case, I swear the ball got there first. Willie—well, he kind of *overtook* it from behind. It was more than a great catch. It was an impossible catch!"

Comparison with DiMaggio inevitably leaped to mind at a time like that, and the Giants had a resident expert in Tommy Henrich, formerly DiMag's teammate, now a Giant coach.

"I think," Heinrich said slowly, "that DiMag *might* have covered that same distance in the same amount of time, and *might* have got a glove on the ball." He took a deep breath. "But he couldn't have caught it."

Heresy? Listen to Joe Gordon. Another of DiMaggio's ex-teammates and a long-time favorite among coast fans, Gordon was frequently asked, at San Francisco baseball banquets, who was the greatest he ever saw. The fans always expected that stock home-town answer: "Joe Di-Maggio."

But when they asked him, early in 1962, Gordon said flatly: "You're not going to like this, but the greatest I ever saw is Willie Mays."

No, Willie's slump of 1956 was a slump only by his own standards. For among other years, that off season was the season he became the first player in history to steal more than 30 bases and hit more than 30 home runs in one and the same year.

In 1957 he was to repeat that feat, and if you are not impressed by small figures like 30, then consider that before the 1959 season had ended, Mays had become the only player in history to hit more than 200 homers and steal more than 200 bases. Furthermore, it seemed likely he was destined to make that not 200 but 300, for going into the 1963 season his career totals were 368 home runs and 241 stolen bases.

The Giants were to finish sixth again in '57, their last season in New York, but Willie Mays was hitting .333, leading the league in triples for the third time in four years (this time with a startling total of 20), becoming the first player in National League history to record 20 or more doubles, triples, and home runs the same season. He had a triple and a single in the All-Star game ("but he was sick," manager Rigney rightly pointed out—it's true, Mays was hobbled by a bad leg).

That year, the defense fanciers had new candidates to add to their choice of Mays catches—one off Bobby Morgan (one of the very few times Willie left his feet to make a catch), another off Bob Skinner (a drive at the Polo Grounds like the Wertz smash, but hit even farther, so that Mays had to catch the ball and dodge an abutment of the bleachers at the same moment).

And on the final day of the 1957 season—the last game at the Polo Grounds—Willie Mays grounded out routinely to shortstop in his last time at bat.

As he came back to the bench, the crowd rose and gave him a standing ovation.

Mays had to blink back the tears. "I never felt so nervous," he has since recalled. "I was trying too hard. My hands were shaking. I wanted to hit a home run, just to show them how I felt. I wanted to do something for the New York fans."

That was nothing more or less than the truth, but those words were to haunt Willie.

For San Francisco is a proud city.

It doesn't take kindly to people who want to do things for New York.

THE NOT-SO-GOLDEN GATE

San Francisco staged a parade for the Giants when they came to town. There was dancing in the streets. Owner Horace Stoneham, manager Bill Rigney, star outfielder Willie Mays were feted and lionized.

Behind this enthusiasm, however, was the truth of the matter, which was that San Francisco was celebrating the fact that it had become "big league." The city was congratulating not the Giants but itself.

The Giants in general, and Mays in particular, were to find this out.

Things that happened—and not all of them by any

means in the Giants' first year in their new town—included
some rather unbelievable items.

Such as:

The city had promised to build a new ball park for the
Giants. When the new park turned out to have alleged
faults, not only in its finished construction but in its
financing and location, Mr. Stoneham—who had little or
nothing to do with it—found himself picking up much of
the blame.

The local press took after the Giants from every con-
ceivable angle. At one point, Stoneham's very patriotism
was questioned by a front-page story that asked why the
Giants refused to fly the American flag at night. (Stoneham had always believed, as most true patriots have believed, that "the sun never sets on the American flag"—
that the flag is to be struck at sundown, except in battle.)
But pressure from this newspaper forced him to fly the
flag at night.

Worst of all, the press and the fans had been accustomed
to minor-league baseball all these years. They did not
understand the subtle but acute differences between the
top minors and the majors. (The fact, for example, that
major league teams carry 25 players, triple-A minor league
teams 21 players, means a world of difference to the number of moves a manager can make during a game, but few
in San Francisco recognized this.)

And since the old San Francisco Seals had had some fine
teams, and since San Francisco had sent more than its
share of fine players up to the big leagues, San Franciscans
were convinced as a result that the way to keep the Giants
from losing in the National League was to apply the

strategy and tactics that had produced winning teams, and winning players, in the Pacific Coast League.

This, of course, was ridiculous. It was to produce some of the funniest advice from sports writers ever to appear in print, but the humor of it was lost because the local people took it seriously. And as a serious result, Giant players and management became leery of talking to fans and writers at precisely the time when such communication was needed between the team and its new city.

Finally, while their new home was being constructed, the Giants played their 1958 and 1959 seasons at Seals Stadium where, in a typical minor league setting, the stands are close to the foul lines and the fans sit practically on top of the players. So the players started hearing abuse which, though no different from the taunts they might receive in established major league cities, still was in this case delivered "personally"—from close range.

Perhaps newspaper executive Frank Conniff summed it up best when he accompanied Soviet Premier Khrushchev during the latter's visit to San Francisco in September of 1959—the height of that year's pennant race. Conniff not only covered his assignment, but also found time to take in a ball game.

"This," he said, as a result, "is the darndest city I ever did see—they cheer Khrushchev and boo Willie Mays!"

For Mays had problems all his own—worse than anyone else's, even Stoneham's.

He was the superstar from New York. Because he represented the "New York" in the Giants, the San Francisco fans resented him on that score. Because of his reputation, he represented of course a threat to San Francisco's fa-

vorite baseball son, who too had played center field—Joe
DiMaggio. (What a piece of irony for the man who, as
a youngster, had pretended he was DiMaggio!) And because he was colored, Mays experienced a few unpleasant
reactions on that score—a house denied to him, a rock
thrown through the window of the house he did occupy.

Before the Giants' first San Francisco season was a
month old, the fans had "shown" Willie Mays. Where,
they wanted to know, were the home runs?

And to his own amazement, Mays found himself being
filmed, via motion picture camera, while at bat. San
Francisco wanted to show him what he was doing wrong.
The funny thing is, he was batting .375 at the time.

He was to go on, that year, to bat .347—his all-time high
—with 35 home runs and the league's base-stealing cham-
pionship. But to talk of "stealing" tells only a part of the
story. Mays by now had become a greater baserunner than
Jackie Robinson. (He had Robinson's instinct and more
than Robinson's speed. To this he now added Robinson's
ability to worry the pitcher. And he had an extra element
all his own—the ability to beat out the slow, or "topped,"
or deep, ground ball for a hit.)

As a result, Mays not only could worry the pitcher—he
could worry the defense too. Worry them into playing
closer to him and therefore out of position for the hitter.
Worry them into hurrying their throws.

It got so bad at one point that as cool and veteran a
customer as Robin Roberts could stand no more. With
Mays on second, he stepped off the pitcher's mound and
literally challenged Willie to a fight! Mays simply had
teased him beyond endurance.

"It was an impulsive thing to do," Roberts confessed

afterward. "An immature thing. I don't know why I did it, but I accused Willie of stealing the catcher's signs. I heard him yelling out there and moving around, and I just went out to tell him about it. It was a foolish thing to do."

Finally, the umpires restored order, and Roberts delivered his next pitch to the Giant hitter. And when the catcher looked up, Mays was already on third!

The Giants had a rookie first baseman that first year, Orlando Cepeda, and San Francisco thought he was wonderful. He was young, he was exciting, he could hit a ball a mile—but most of all, he was new.

He had no connection with New York.

Mays batted third in the Giant order most of that year; Cepeda batted fourth.

Cepeda batted .312, with 25 homers (to Mays' 29); 96 rbi's (Mays also had 96); 4 triples (Mays had 11).

It is that .312 batting average that fascinated baseball men. Most of them agreed it would have been less than .300 except for the fact of the Giant batting order—Mays batting third, Cepeda batting fourth.

Willie was on first base so often that year, and his threat as a runner was so pronounced, that time and again Cepeda *knew* in advance what the pitch was going to be! It would have to be a fast ball—for if it was anything less than a fast ball, it would be an invitation to Mays to steal.

Cepeda himself has been the first to acknowledge Mays' contribution to his first year in the majors. "He helped me every way a man can help another man," Orlando said. "He put points on my batting average. He taught me plays. He even kept me from a lot of trouble."

The last was a reference to an episode in Pittsburgh,

when the explosive Cepeda took off after Pirate manager Danny Murtaugh with a bat. Mays tackled Orlando—a flying-type football tackle—and sat on him till things cooled down a bit.

But when all was said and done, at the end of 1958—the Giants had finished third—Cepeda, not Mays, was the poll choice of the San Francisco fans as "most valuable Giant."

"CALL IT HYPNOSIS"

In 1959, the Giants came awfully close to a pennant. They wound up finishing third again, but they actually had a two game lead over the rest of the league with just eight games to go. Then, suddenly, they couldn't win for losing, and that was that.

Sullenly, once more, San Francisco decided the trouble was that nobody connected with the Giant organization knew how to play winning baseball.

For Mays, that season, there were 82 extra-base hits, including 43 doubles and 34 homers. And there was something that happened that made him even more than a complete ballplayer.

Something? Something extra? Something else?

What was left for him to do that he hadn't done already?

"Call it hypnosis," manager Rigney said, adding: "I don't know what else you'd call it."

The story—and it's quite a story—dates back to 1954, just before Mays "quit" hitting homers on Leo Durocher's orders. Willie's 35th home run that year was hit at least 500 feet, as far back into the deep-set left-field upper deck at the Polo Grounds as it is possible to hit a ball. And it was still going up when it struck the rear wall of the stand.

By Willie's own account, this was the longest homer he had ever hit, up until that time.

The strange thing was that it came off a "change-up"—a slow pitch thrown low and outside by Harvey Haddix, then with the Cardinals.

Now, a baseball is essentially a rubber ball—it has a rubber center. This means that the harder it is thrown, the farther it will travel when it hits something, regardless of what that something is—a brick wall, a dirt infield, or a bat.

As a result, almost all long hits—the home runs that are measured at 450 feet or more—come off fast balls.

But Mays had hit his 500-footer off a change-up! Which means he had to supply most of the power!

Mr. Haddix, a thoughtful soul, remembered that.

He remembered it year in and year out, and in all their meetings never threw Willie that pitch again—until one July day in 1959 at Pittsburgh, when with two out in the eighth, and with the Pirates leading by one run, and with a Giant on base, and with Mays at bat, Haddix tried that pitch one more time.

Mays socked it over the left field fence to win the game.

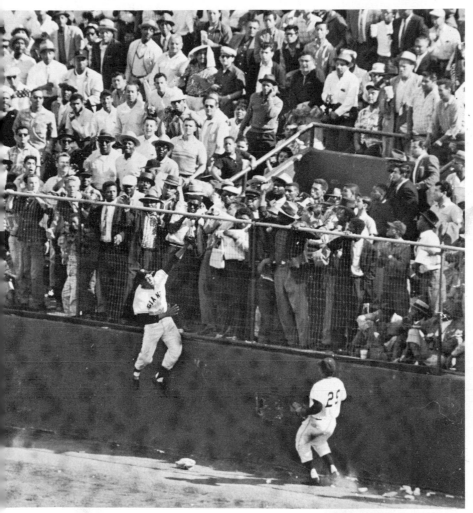

An airborne Willie Mays sails high against the right center-field wall in San Francisco pennant race of 1959. Willie missed the catch, and by season's end the Giants had missed another pennant.

He had waited five years for one pitch.

What did that do to Mr. Haddix?

Well, sir, next time the Pirates played the Giants, it was in San Francisco, in August, 1959, and the teams were tied 3–3, and in the last of the eighth Haddix struck out the first two Giants to face him.

Now it was Mays' turn to bat.

Haddix called time and summoned manager Murtaugh from the Pittsburgh dugout.

"What's the matter?" Murtaugh asked.

"I want to walk him," Haddix said.

"You want to *what*?"

"Walk him."

"But you've got bases empty. If he gets on, he'll steal second."

"I'd rather have him on first and pitch the percentage against the next hitter. Don't worry about him stealing. I'm left-handed. I can hold him on."

That was it. Haddix did not want to pitch to Mays.

Murtaugh didn't put up too much of a fight. For all he knew, Haddix might be right—maybe Mays did have his number, and putting him on first base in this situation might be less harmful than letting him swing—unorthodox though the idea was.

So the Pirate manager shrugged and went back to the bench, and Haddix proceeded to issue an intentional pass to Mays with bases empty and two out.

Now it was the turn of the Giants' new rookie sensation of that year, Willie McCovey, to hit.

Manager Rigney called him over from the on-deck circle.

"Don't swing at the ball till Willie's on second," Rigney instructed.

On the third pitch Mays stole second.

On the fourth pitch McCovey singled to center to score him and win the game for the Giants.

Since that time, box score after box score show the Pirates taking Haddix out of the game rather than permitting him to pitch to Mays in an important situation!

"Call it hypnosis," Rigney had said.

That same year, 1959, Mays won the All-Star game with a triple to deepest right-center field. Writer Bob Stevens coined a famous descriptive line about that memorable hit: "The only man who could have caught it," Stevens wrote, "hit it."

That same year Mays came down with a hip injury. He was resting on the bench, but Rigney needed him to pinch hit. Mays was at bat when the Giant who was on second base at the time got himself picked off. Now Mays singled, and—bad hip and all—stole second.

The next night the hip hurt even worse. Again, Rigney rested Willie, but again needed him for the pinch hit late in the game. This time Mays homered.

"You know what I think?" said writer James McGee. "I think he homered on purpose that time—so he wouldn't have to run!"

Now, finally, it became 1960. The fans in San Francisco still hadn't warmed up to Willie, but things kept getting better. And for the first time, the city had a major-league ball park—Candlestick Park.

Maybe that would change some things.

The Giants didn't get a chance to see Candlestick till

the day before the season opened. It was a raw, cold day, and the wind whipped in from left field.

Dale Long was the first Giant to step into the batter's box. Long is a left-handed hitter. The first pitch he saw, he hit out of the park.

"Looks like you'll have fun here," an onlooker said to Mays.

"I don't know," Willie said. "I don't like that wind for *nothing!*"

"But Long just hit a home run."

"He's a left-handed hitter. I'm right-handed."

"Well," the onlooker said, "a wind is a wind. They've got wind other places too."

"Maybe not quite like here," Willie said, and he stepped in to take his licks.

He swung at the first pitch, then stepped back, a look of disbelief on his face. In his hand was half a bat.

A combination of the kind of pitch, the climate, and that "not-quite-like-here" wind had sawed the bat in two!

THE END OF SOMETHING

The tip-off on Candlestick Park in its first season, 1960, was Mays' total of extra-base hits that year: 70, his lowest full-season total since coming to the majors. This despite a .319 batting average and 29 homers (most of it, and them, built in road parks).

Willie had another reason for liking to play away from San Francisco: the fans were friendlier (particularly so in Philadelphia, where hundreds of New Yorkers would ride the trains down to watch the Giants play).

"The fans were friendlier"—that does not mean they did not like him in San Francisco. It does mean that he had the feeling they liked him in San Francisco because he was a part of San Francisco's team. On the road, they loved him for himself.

If anything was needed to reinforce this state of mind, it was the way they "got" Bill Rigney.

For a long time, certain people in San Francisco wanted to see one of their own native sons—a fine baseball great named Lefty O'Doul—made manager of the Giants. There was nothing wrong with this ambition by itself. There was a great deal wrong with the way they went about it.

To get O'Doul, they first had to get rid of Rigney. Since Rigney was doing a good job (it was mid-June, and the Giants were in second place), they had to invent a reason.

They were reasonably certain that president Stoneham would go along with their wishes, not because he agreed with them, but because he was still new in San Francisco's world, and had to knuckle under for the sake of long-term good will.

But first, again to repeat, they had to invent a reason. And they found one.

The rumor began to spread that the great Willie Mays wouldn't play for Rigney! That he had asked to be benched!

Completely outside his own control, Mays had been made an instrument of Rigney's dismissal. And it worked, too. Rig was fired.

Stoneham would not go so far as to hire O'Doul, however. As long-time manager of the San Francisco Seals of the Pacific Coast League, O'Doul was accustomed to handling players not of his own choosing. Stoneham felt the Giants needed a manager familiar with present-day major-league personnel—one who was prepared to select players as well as teach them. Teaching, after all, was not all there was to big-league baseball—though sometimes it is the major part of minor-league baseball.

So, as an interim move, Stoneham appointed his own

chief scout, Tom Sheehan, to pilot the club for the rest of 1960. It was so obviously an interim move that the club reacted accordingly—rudderless, you might call it—and finished in fifth place.

But for Mays, it was the end of something.

The papers had made it look like he had been instrumental in the firing of Rigney—and nothing was farther from the truth.

Far from not wanting to play for Rig, Willie had—unknown to the public—played the final six weeks of 1959 with a broken finger, and paced the team every inch of the way.

"If you can't play for him, you can't play for anybody," was his tribute to Bill Rigney.

But Willie's voice was not enough.

And he had been used, used by persons bent on gaining their own ends.

It was quite a season, that 1960. Wrote Arnold Hano:

You can pin down where Mays had his trouble. He hit .299 in San Francisco, and a rousing .338 on the road. He had 12 home runs at home, and 17 away. Mays just couldn't hit through that wind.

The wind played weird tricks. Wally Moon said that balls hit to left field acted like they were on rubber bands. They just stopped in midair and bounced back toward the infield. Don Blasingame said the wind made pop-fly hitters out of strong right-handed batters, which didn't explain why it also made a pop-fly hitter out of left-handed Don Blasingame. Charley Dressen wanted to know how much it would cost to put a dome on top. He complained that the wind even affected pitched balls and made it hard for the umpire to follow them, which was the first time Dressen had been known to admit umpires ever did follow pitches. Pittsburgh's Don Hoak swore the wind moved ground balls sidewise, and Jim Marshall suggested starting games at eight in the morning because it wasn't so windy then (just foggy). The Giants were assured that the wind would die down in June, so on June 11, Orlando Cepeda, after being called out on strikes, threw his helmet in the air, and the wind carried it ten rows into the seats.

So there was the wind at Candlestick, and the bad managerial situation, yet, somehow, Willie still wanted to win!

Does that sound obvious to you?

Well, the truth is that some of the Giants that year *weren't* too concerned with winning.

It was too easy to tread water, to see where the land lay. If Tom Sheehan was an interim manager, it meant the Giant front office had given up on a pennant for '60. Why should the working man—the player—do any more?

The ones who did do more were the exception, not the rule.

One of them happened to be Mays.

One of his trademarks—streaky performance at bat—was there for all to see in '60. In late May he slumped at the plate, collecting but one single in 20 times at bat. Then, in his next 12 games, Willie was over .400, with production that included five doubles, a triple, and six home runs. In that stretch, Willie scored 15 runs, drove in 16.

"Even when they got him out he was hitting the ball on the nose," Giant official John Taddeucci said. "I never saw anything like it."

The fans believed Mays was a streak hitter—how could they help it with such proof before them?—and Mays himself believed it. Yet it is not so significant a thing as it may seem. Almost all good hitters are streak types. Knowing their own capabilities, they tend to tighten, to over-correct, when they go, say, eight times without a hit, and this tends to prolong the dry spell. Also, a good hitter will have his share of hard-hit balls taken away from him by classy fielding plays, and when these episodes come bunched together, as the law of averages says will happen from time to time, the same goose eggs go into the box score, just as though the batter had struck out.

Finally, streaks can be deceiving. Mays has had one 15-game hitting streak, tops for the Giants that season, in which he got nothing but singles, usually one a game and that one not well hit, and during which his batting average dropped more than 10 points! On another occasion, as we saw in 1951, he got just six hits over one spell, but all six were homers.

The interesting thing about Mays and his streaks, however, is Willie's ability to compensate. "When he's not hitting," Leo Durocher has said, "he's doing something else to beat you." The meaning behind those artless words has depth. Durocher was saying that Mays, time and again, seems actually to make up for dry periods at bat by doing something else particularly well.

When you stop to think about it, this is definitely the mark of a certain kind of player—and just as definitely not the mark of the other kind. You've all seen players who seemed to slump "all over" at the same time. Suddenly and simultaneously, it would appear they not only couldn't get a hit at bat but couldn't pick up the ball in the field.

But take Mays during that hitting slump of his in 1960.

In a Memorial Day double header against the Cubs at Candlestick Park, Willie in the first game made two of his greatest catches. One of the two, pictured on page 8, came on a sharp, fading liner to right center from the bat of Ed Bouchee and is the personal favorite of some Mays followers as his most beautiful catch of all time. As the picture shows, Mays timed his stride, body position, and the extra reach of a glove held nearly *off the hand*, to snatch the ball when it *had* to be past him for a triple!

But the Giants lost the first game of that double header. In the last half of the ninth inning in the second game, Mays was on first—he wasn't hitting, so he'd drawn a walk —and, holding the first baseman close with his lead, he opened up the hole through which McCovey now drove a routine single to right field.

Mays whirled around to third, but he had a notion too— for sure enough, the right fielder had thrown the ball to the second baseman (a normal enough play). And in that instant, Willie Mays just kept going.

Flustered, the second basemen threw home—a bad throw, up the line, and Mays scored the winning run.

What if it had been a good throw?

He probably would have scored anyway, kicking the ball out of the catcher's grasp if necessary. For Mays had sized up his opposition and knew that the outfielder, second baseman, and catcher all were rookies and could be subject to the pressures of a make-or-break play.

Furthermore, after eight hours of baseball, Willie summed it all up later when he said, "It was time to go home."

Scoring from first on a single is not usually done; frequently, those times that you do see it, the run is not that important. Yet in this case, knowing in advance that he was the only target runner, Mays knew, through instinctive compilation of all the factors involved, that this was the right play.

"Kick the ball out of the catcher's grasp?" Such a claim is made above. Willie has done that too. In a game at Cincinnati one recent season, the score was 0–0 in the top of the seventh. The Giants had one out, bases loaded, and Ed Bailey at bat. Bailey grounded to Cincinnati first baseman Gordon Coleman two steps from the base. Coleman stepped on first, then threw home. That meant there were now two out, but it also took the force off the play at the plate. The catcher—again, a rookie, just as Coleman at first, didn't have too much major-league experience—had to tag the Giant runner coming from third. The Giant runner was Mays.

Of Coleman's decision to touch first before throwing home, one writer said:

> This was clearly the right play—unless you want to say that catcher Jerry Zimmerman had caught only a dozen games in his major-league lifetime, and that the greatest baserunner in the game was bearing down on him. And here in the seventh inning of a scoreless tie, you were choosing a tag play on Mays instead of the more simple force.
>
> Oh, Mama, did Willie hit him! Zimmerman and the ball traveled together about six feet through the air. Then Zimmerman stopped and the ball kept going. Once the recovery had been made, [Orlando] Cepeda was across the plate too and [Jim] Davenport was on

third, whence he scored a moment later on a deft swinging drag to the left of the mound by the adroit Jose
Pagan. . . .

The Reds had made the right play, but on the wrong
man. Right then and there, Willie Mays broke open the
ball game.

Following the 1960 season—that year of that terrible
wind at Candlestick, and the bad situation Mays found
himself in, wherein he was used to force Rigney's removal
as manager; that year of "streaks" and "only" 70 extra-
base hits—president Stoneham called Mays into his office
for a chat.

"Willie," Stoneham said, "to begin with, we're raising
your salary. Again."

This time, the raise was to $85,000!

"And," the clubowner went on, "we're going to put up
a green backdrop back of the center field fence at Candlestick, to help the hitters follow the pitches; and we're
going to pull the fences in a little; and we're going to start
day games at one instead of one-thirty, so we can get an
extra half hour in before the wind comes up."

Mays liked that as much as his raise in salary.

"Wait," Stoneham said. "The best is yet to come. Know
who's your new manager?"

"Who?"

"Who helped you the most, on the field, when you were
new with the Giants in New York?"

"Dark," Mays said.

"That's who it is," Stoneham said.

THE BEGINNING OF
SOMETHING

Mays called Dark "Cap," a salute to the old days in New York when shortstop Dark also was team captain of the Giants. Indeed, that first day of spring training at Phoenix in 1961 was a playback of ten years earlier, for not only Dark and Mays, but coaches Larry Jansen, Whitey Lockman and Wes Westrum all combined to give the Giants five men who actually had been in the lineup when Bobby Thomson hit his well-remembered home run.

Of course, of the five, only Mays was still active, but Dark didn't mind surrounding himself with reminders of the Giant pennant years of the 1950s. "The new manager," one writer said, "is looking for old ways to win games instead of new ways to lose them."

The relationship between Alvin Dark and Willie Mays, always a warm one, was to blossom to new heights now. Dark even went so far as to make the statement in a radio interview that "without Mays, the Giants are a very ordinary team." This may sound rather obvious and non-controversial except that the unforgiving San Francisco press thought the manager had no business talking that way in public.

Mays, in his turn, told a friend, "I never thought I'd say this about anybody, but I think more of Cap than I did of Leo."

It was a new cast of characters—pitchers like O'Dell, Miller, Sanford, McCormick, Marichal; catchers like Bailey and Haller; a new second base-shortstop combination of Charley Hiller and Jose Pagan; the Alou brothers, Matty and Felipe; and some of the other regular holdovers from the Rigney regime, like third baseman Davenport, and first baseman-outfielders Cepeda and McCovey.

And, fresh from a trade with the Cleveland club of the American League, the veteran utility star, Harvey Kuenn.

It didn't take Kuenn long to learn about Willie Mays.

In an exhibition game at Palm Springs, Harvey was on first and Dark flashed the hit-and-run sign to Mays, who was at bat. In came the pitch—right at Willie's head. He tumbled flat on his back, but somehow, in the act, his bat was still protecting the runner. The ball shot on a searing, low line all the way to the left-field wall for a triple.

Kuenn came around the bases alternately laughing and muttering to himself. "He hits it while he's lying on his back in the dirt, and I score from first base," Harvey said later. "I just want to tell you something. I've heard a lot about this guy. Okay. He just made a believer out of me."

Mays made a believer out of Maury Wills, the fastest man in the league, the first time the Giants played at Los Angeles in 1961. We have talked about some of Willie's great throws—the throw against Colavito in that exhibition game, mentioned in Chapter Five; "The Throw" on Cox in the 1951 season; a throw from deepest right-center field at St. Louis that got Joe Cunningham at the plate in 1954. After the St. Louis play, *The New York Times* asked Russ Hodges if he would mind letting them put a man with him in the broadcasting booth for a few days to see whether Hodges was exaggerating or not when he described Willie's plays (Hodges said yes, and the *Times* man came away from his assignment saying simply: "He doesn't exaggerate.")

But this one on Wills at Los Angeles in '61 ranked with the best of them. It was a high liner to center, and Mays snatched the ball out of the air and, with Wills streaking for the plate after the catch, put the ball in catcher Tom Haller's glove with a throw that not only was in time to get Wills but insured he could not touch the plate, so perfectly was the ball aimed into the plate-blocking stance of the catcher. "He couldn't have thrown it better," manager Dark said afterward, "if he'd walked to the plate, surveyed the situation, and *placed* the ball in Haller's mitt!"

It was at the next port of call on that road trip, Milwaukee, that the next triumph of Willie Mays took place.

There is a story behind it. Ordinarily Mays rooms by himself. His habits on the field are (showmanship to one side) essentially quiet—he has never once been thrown out of a game by an umpire. His habits off the field are equally quiet. Some rock 'n' roll records on the portable phonograph he sometimes carries with him—a Western movie or two at the local Bijou—these, together with a lot of sleep, satisfy Willie.

So circumspect is he, in fact, that an idea came to manager Dark. On this road swing, early in '61, he decided to room Mays with Willie McCovey, as a means of bringing a calming influence to McCovey, who was not above a 2 A.M. snack of barbequed ribs.

The idea backfired.

Here in Milwaukee, the night of Saturday, April 29, McCovey brought a double order of ribs to the room in the post-midnight calm. Mays happily pitched in.

An hour later, Mays was wickedly, violently sick. Doc Bowman, the team trainer, had to come to the room and let him have some medicine to calm his stomach and make him sleep.

On top of that, Mays was in one of his slumps. Friday night, Warren Spahn had pitched a no-hitter against the Giants. Saturday, the Giants had exploded for a 7–3 win, on 15 hits, but Mays had none of the 15. (He had made a sensational catch, but that's par for his course. He still wasn't hitting.)

Next day, a Sunday, there was doubt whether Mays would play.

A writer friend, one of the few San Francisco writers Mays trusted, sat down beside him in front of his locker in the clubhouse before the game.

"How do you feel, Willie?" the writer asked.

"Weak as a cat," Willie said.

"Going to play today?"

"Going to try, I guess."

"Well," the writer friend said, "don't press too hard."

Mays looked at him. "Press too hard? You writing I'm in a slump?"

"Not the way you put it, no."

"Everybody else is."

"No they're not."

"I'll come out of it," Mays said. "I always do."

"You'll come out of it faster," the writer said, "if you stop thinking you're in it to begin with. The worst thing about your streaks is you think they've got to happen. You go oh-for-six, you say to yourself, 'I'm in a streak. I won't get a hit the next 15 times at bat.' There's no law says this has to be this way. You make them worse by talking yourself into them."

"I know," Willie Mays said. "I know." He grinned at the writer. "What do you do when *you* get in a slump?"

"I never have slumps," the writer said, stiffly.

Mays began to laugh. "I read you," he said. "I know you get your slumps, same's rest of us."

"Well," the writer said, "if I do get into a slump, sooner or later I come out of it. That's the best I can tell you. I don't know how."

Mays grinned. "Same's with me," he said. "Quit worrying. I'll get me four hits in a game and be right back up there. Don't you worry about nothing."

"Listen," the writer said testily, "*I'm* not worrying. You make me sound like *I* got to go up there and hit Burdette today. I know you're going to come out of it. You'll come out of it faster when you quit eating spareribs at midnight, that's all."

Mays began to laugh. "Don't go 'way mad," he said.

And that day, April 30, 1961, he did get four hits, just as he said he might.

All four were home runs.

HIS GREATEST DAY

Four home runs in one game. How do you top that? Mays found a way.

The date: June 29, 1961. The place: Philadelphia.

It was the Giants' second trip of '61 to Philly. The first time, Mays had scored from first on a routine single to left field! It so demoralized the Phils that the next day the Giants won again, this time by a score of 7–0, even though they were out-hit. You figure out a way of getting fewer hits than the other team, yet still shutting them out 7–0!

The June trip to Philadelphia resulted in a weird series of games. First the Phillies won 1–0, with the Giants leaving eight runners in scoring position, and Alvin Dark was so wrought up he tore off a piece of finger throwing a stool in the clubhouse afterward. Then, the night of June 28, the two teams played to a 15-inning, 7–7 tie in the longest night game in major league history—five hours, 11 minutes.

As a result, the next day—actually, it was the same day—they had to replay the tie game as part of a twilight-night double header.

In the first game, Mays had three home runs and a single, batting in five runs. One of the homers, the last one, came in the tenth inning and spelled an 8–7 Giant victory.

In the second game, the Giants won 4–1. Mays walked, doubled, and tripled, scored twice, batted in a pair. His total for the double header was, therefore, six hits for 18 total bases.

He had never, despite his gaudy career in home runs, hit so many as three homers in one game before this season. Now he had done it twice—the four at Milwaukee, now the three in the first game of tonight's twin bill.

But there was more to it than that. In the first inning of the second game, two errors enabled the fleet Tony Taylor of the Phillies to reach third base with one out.

Billy Loes was the Giant pitcher, and Billy was about ready to chuck the whole thing over. Earlier in this story, you may remember, mention was made of Mays misjudging a fly ball. That had happened the previous week, and Loes was the pitcher at the time, and that, plus three other bad fielding plays by the Giants, so upset Loes that he stalked off the field.

But it was said, remember, that Mays made up for his lapse. Tonight in Philadelphia was the time and place. Here was Loes, ready to "blow" again, and coming back of that frazzled week of baseball, manager Dark had no one else left to pitch.

At this point, with Taylor on third, came a re-creation of Mays' famous throw on Maury Wills. It was the same kind of ball—the high liner—and Taylor was, like Wills, a speedster. But here came that ball to the plate and: double play, inning over. And Billy Loes went on to pitch a five-hitter.

Long-time Giant official Garry Schumacher refers to this double header as Mays' greatest day in baseball.

"He did everything the complete ballplayer can do," Schumacher said. "He hit for average, he hit for distance. He caught the ball. He threw it. He ran the bases—after that walk in the second game he took second base on what they called a passed ball, but no one else would have been going on it. He personally won both ends of a double header for a team that was completely worn out. We had one man left who could pitch, and Willie personally kept him on the rails and in the game. It had to be his greatest day."

As well it might have been, though Mays would vote for another day. Just as in Philadelphia, this one wasn't a "day"—it was a night: the night of July 24. Just as the eastern fans, as seen in Philadelphia, most appreciated Mays, so it was this night, for this was the occasion of the Giants' return to New York—for an exhibition game with the Yankees.

The San Francisco *Examiner's* story of that night told how 50,000 fans turned out in the rain to see the Giants at Yankee Stadium:

The Giants had come home, and in a driving, steaming summer rainstorm, the big town turned out to say hello.

There was no pregame practice. It was raining. The pregame home-run contest (Cepeda and Mays for us, Mantle and Maris for them) was called off. It was raining.

Game time was held up half an hour past the scheduled 7:55 P.M. start.

"We'll never play tonight," Alvin Dark said.

"Look outside and you'll change your mind," he was told.

He went down the runway and up into the visiting dugout along the third-base line and looked.

"Wow," he said reverently.

There in the rain sat the people. Waiting.

It went back to misting, and the game went on.

"Ladies and Gentlemen," said the Yankee Stadium announcer, giving the lineup for the San Francisco Giants, "at second base, number *14*, Joe Amalfitano."

The cheering started.

"Number *7*, Harvey Kuenn, right field. . . ."

It got louder.

"Number *41*, Matty Alou, left field. . . ."

Louder and louder.

"Number *24*, Wil——"

You never heard the rest of the Giant batting order announced here tonight.

An unbroken, throat-swelling peal of adulation sprang from the hearts of Giant-starved New Yorkers. It rolled and volleyed off the great tiering of this triple-decked palace and against the vague outline of the Bronx County courthouse, looming in the gray-black mist out beyond the huge scoreboard in right center-field.

They rocked and tottered and shouted and stamped and sang. It was joy and love and welcome, and you never heard a cascade of sound quite like it. . . .

The other San Francisco papers had similar stories. All the stories definitely agreed on one point—that this would never happen in San Francisco.

"IT CAN GET TO YOU"

For Mays in 1961, there were 40 homers, 123 runs batted in—his greatest totals since coming West—and 129 runs scored, a league-leading figure and his all-time personal high.

For the Giants, there was a third-place finish and a winter trade bringing them veteran front-line pitchers Don Larsen and Billy Pierce.

"This is going to be the year," Alvin Dark said. He was talking of 1962.

For the first time, the National League had ten teams: now it would be a 162-game schedule, instead of the old 154, and Dark said he planned to rest his front-liners, Mays in particular, every chance he got.

"It can get to you," the manager said. "I know how it is."

His first time at bat in 1962, Willie Mays hit a home run off Warren Spahn.

And the Giants were off and running.

One of the most reliable rules in baseball is that the team that is hot in September the year before will start hot the next season. The Giants in '61 won 15 ball games in the last three weeks of the campaign, during which time they played mostly against first-division competition.

They'd been hot, and next season they started hot. In '62, they won 40 of their first 55 games.

But how do you rest a Willie Mays who was leading the league in home runs from opening day on?

Dark's Giants were to play all year long at a percentage better than any Giant team in 51 years. But the Dodgers, feasting on the weak clubs, would be ahead of them most of the time.

"There are 25 players on the Giants," said Bob Stevens of the San Francisco *Chronicle*, "but you can begin and end with *24*." *24*—that was Mays. "Willie Mays," Stevens said, in a short sentence that said it all, "is the Giants!"

He beat Casey Stengel's New York Mets one day in San Francisco with a home run in the tenth inning, but Casey was unimpressed. "It wasn't the one in the tenth that wowed me," he said afterward. "It was the one he hit in the eighth—he hit that one one-handed!"

Mays was to hit "only" .304 in 1962. But his slugging average would reach a point where its lifetime total now was the greatest in the history of the National League—for any player, any number of years. He led both leagues in home runs with 49, totaled a new team record of 90 extra-base hits, still—at the age of thirty-one—led his club with his "usual" 19 stolen bases, drew 78 walks, scored a new career high of 130 runs, batted in a nice number: 141!

The combination of hitting for distance and hitting for average never was so clearly shown as in the Mays of '62, and the significance is pointed up by an old truism—you can't hit .300 without getting singles. Mays had 99 singles, 90 extra-base hits. Here was a balance of average and power that some players have equaled—a Musial, a Di-Maggio—but when you add to those figures the fact that more than half of those 90 extra-base hits were home runs, then you have squared the circle. *Nobody* hits like that!

Yet in 1962 Willie Mays was tired, and Willie Mays was troubled. His marriage in 1956 now had resulted in divorce, costing him the companionship of his three-year-old adopted son Michael. The new schedule of day-in, day-out competition added to his burdens. There was one all-but-unnoticed additional fact: in 1962, the Giants were rained out only twice, in games made up immediately the following day. Too much rain can hurt a club, by piling up the double headers. But nobody ever considered the effects of too little rain! What happened was that, day in, day out, the Giants played.

And Willie Mays carried them. In '51 he was an inspiration to his team; in '54 he was the star. But he was younger then, and he looked up to the other players. In '62 he was the "elder statesman." The team looked to him.

There were other things—unlooked-for things. In one game against the Mets, Mays found himself in the midst of a major brawl on the field. Elio Chacon, the New York second baseman, was trying to trap Willie off second. Four times, pitcher Roger Craig threw, and all four times, Mays was back safely (of course—manager Dark had said he *never* saw Willie picked off second). And finally Chacon could stand no more, and started throwing punches.

It was an unequal contest. Willie picked Chacon up and dropped him into short-center field. And when pitcher Craig acted as if he wanted to get into it, a large man named Cepeda trotted over to him and suggested that he change his mind. Mr. Craig agreed that was a good idea.

The Mets played at the Polo Grounds in '62, and the Giants' first trip there was another memory event, like the exhibition game against the Yankees the year before. This, though, wasn't exhibition play. A Met pitcher named Miller struck Willie out three times. The fourth time, Mays hit the ball farther than he'd hit that one off Haddix in '54. Russ Hodges didn't have time to say "Bye-bye baby." He didn't have time to say "Good-bye." All he had time to say, when Willie hit this one, was "Oh, no!" Then, briefly, and unnecessarily, Hodges added: "That's gone!"

Mays was the star as the Giants took three out of four from the Dodgers in Los Angeles at the beginning of September. Now the ball club went on the road, having won seven in a row, with a won-and-lost mark of 94 and 51. They trailed the Dodgers by just half a game.

The road trip opened in Cincinnati—a night game there on a hot, muggy evening. In the top half of the second inning, Russ Hodges told his San Francisco audience—and all San Francisco was listening—"There's some commotion in the Giant dugout."

Then, Hodges said: "They're bringing a stretcher to the dugout."

And then he said the rest of it.

"Willie Mays has collapsed."

ALVIN'S KIND OF TEAM

It was exhaustion, physical and mental, plain and simple.

They put Willie in the hospital in Cincinnati, and the doctor in charge found that he tested normal but that it still wasn't "right" for a thirty-one-year-old athlete to conk out like that. Which, of course, was all that doctor *could* say. Not knowing Mays' background or history, he could hardly take it upon himself to say what the tests showed—that there was nothing wrong. Suppose he'd said Mays could play the next night and Willie had collapsed again?

Had Mays been less perfectly conditioned—he doesn't drink, doesn't smoke, hasn't varied from his playing

weight of 183 pounds as much as two pounds in ten years
—he might have collapsed, under the weight of this tension
and pressure, earlier and more seriously.

But the San Francisco press had a field day.

They printed "rumors."

One said he'd had a heart attack.

Another said he'd had an epileptic seizure.

Another said he was an alcoholic.

And San Francisco's leading columnist printed as his
major rumor of the day the report that Willie had been
hit by a teammate!

What teammate was going to hit Mays?

I called this columnist on the phone and asked him. He
furnished the name of the teammate. You would not
believe it if I printed it here, and I do not propose to
dignify it even to the extent of denying it.

Let's just say instead that here was an epileptic alcoholic,
in the midst of a cardiac seizure, and that a teammate
chose that moment to hit him. Is that silly enough?

What happened to the Giants then was that they lost
six straight.

Alvin Dark said, "I didn't know there could be weeks
like this."

Mays missed that first game, from the second inning on,
and three more games. He got back into action at Pittsburgh on September 16. The Giants were four games off
the pace by then. Willie came up in the eighth inning with
two men on, the score 4–1 against the Giants, two out, and
a pinch hitter, Cepeda, having failed before him. Willie
homered to tie the score at 4–4.

The Giants lost.

Next game, at St. Louis, Mays homered to bring his club
from behind to ahead. They stayed ahead and won.

Game after that, he singled, then scored from first on a bunt play to put his team ahead. An inning later he walked, stole second, continued to third on a short over-throw, and remained there while two teammates struck out. Someone may have had a premonition about those strike-outs. St. Louis third baseman Ken Boyer, for instance, abandoned his ordinary fielding spot and stationed himself on third—simply to keep Mays from stealing home. And the Giants went on to lose.

In Houston, next port of call, Mays got four hits to pace one victory. Then he homered in the eighth inning of the next game—after earlier having gone from second to third on a routine fly ball to *left* field, to be in position to score another run—and he put the Giants ahead 5–4 in the eighth. They lost 6–5 in the ninth.

Back home at San Francisco, the Giants beat the Cardinals twice. Mays batted in the tying run in one game and scored the winning run in the other.

And on the final Sunday of that final week, he stepped to bat in the first inning—and was booed by the San Francisco fans!

He'd gone hitless against Houston in a double header the day before, a double header the Giants split, leaving them one game back of the Dodgers on the morning of the last day.

Yet it was Alvin's kind of team!

They'd fought and won, and they'd fought and lost, and they trailed by four games with seven to go—yet, with the Dodgers losing more than they did, here it was the last day and they still had a chance.

The point was, they'd never given up.

Leo's teams won when they could win.

Alvin's team was to win when it *couldn't!*

The score was Giants 1, Houston 1, in the last half of the eighth inning that final Sunday at Candlestick Park. Willie Mays stepped up to bat. He smashed the ball into the left-field seats to bring the Giants a 2–1 victory.

And the Dodgers lost to the Cardinals, 1–0, and suddenly, at the last moment, the truly impossible had happened: it was 1951 all over again.

CHAPTER
TWENTY-NINE

"WE WANT WILLIE!"

Another play-off, with the first game at Candlestick Park, and in his first time at bat, Mays homered for two runs to launch an 8–0 Giant victory and a perfect day at bat (homer/single/homer/walk—he also stole a base and made an important Mays-type catch).

In the second game, at Los Angeles, the Giants built up a 5–0 lead. But the bull pen failed, and the Dodgers came on to win it.

And in the ninth inning of the third and final game, again at Los Angeles, the Giants went in trailing 4–2.

What was it Leo Durocher had said, so many years ago, as the Giants came to the bench for their final time at bat in that final play-off game of '51?

"Well," he said, sort of reflectively, "you've come this far. It's an awful long way to come. And you've still got a chance to hit."

That Giant team, at that moment, had won 97 out of 156 games.

This 1962 Giant team had won 102 out of 164.

Now it was the turn of Alvin Dark, who had singled to lead off that four-run ninth for the Giants in '51, to be a "Durocher."

Over behind third base, in the Dodger dugout, the real Durocher was now a Dodger coach. But he remembered, too. He was shouting, razzing, teasing—the same old Durocher. Maybe, though, a little of the luster was lost. Perhaps he remembered shouting at Mays in 1961, and having Willie look at him scornfully for one long moment —then hit the ball out of sight for the game-winning homer. Perhaps he was aware that now, in 1962, the Giants had beaten the Dodgers seven of the last nine games they had played. Perhaps he felt the Dodgers should have won it by now (everybody else felt that way).

But Leo was Leo and Alvin was Alvin. Leo had had one set of words to say to his players before that fateful ninth inning 11 years ago. Alvin had another.

What Dark said was brief, concise, to the point.

For this was his kind of team, not Leo's or anybody else's.

What Alvin Dark said was:

"Matty, get your bat."

That's all he said.

And Matty Alou went up to pinch-hit for the pitcher.

Dark's reasoning was strategically sound. He wanted one man—either Matty Alou or Harvey Kuenn, due up next—

to get on base. That way, he could pinch-hit for Charley Hiller with Willie McCovey. The Dodgers could not "percentage" a left-handed pitcher into the game to face McCovey at that point, because the next three Giant hitters—Felipe Alou, Mays, Cepeda—were right-handed.

That's how Dark had it figured.

And Matty Alou did the job. He singled to right.

Kuenn forced him, but now pinch hitter McCovey drew a walk, and Felipe Alou did the same.

Willie Mays was up now with bases loaded.

He slashed a wicked drive up the middle. It hit pitcher Ed Roebuck on the leg and went for a one-run single.

Cepeda got the fly ball to right to score the tying run.

Then, with two out, the new Dodger pitcher, Stan Williams, moved Felipe Alou and Mays up with a wild pitch. Now he had to complete an intentional pass to Ed Bailey to reload the bases.

And then, completely unintentionally, Williams walked Jim Davenport to force the lead run across. The Giants led 5–4.

A Dodger error provided another run, making it 6–4, but that was anticlimactic.

Eleven years to the day, in distance of time, the Giants had again scored four runs in the ninth inning of the last play-off game to defeat the Dodgers and win the pennant.

Mays? His single was, if you review it, the key hit of the inning. He was the only man to both score and bat in a run in the winning rally.

What a contrast to 1951, when, probably to his own benefit, he didn't even come to bat!

The Dodgers were three up, three down in their half of the ninth.

The last out was a routine fly ball to Mays.

He gave it that old pound-the-glove, basket-catch routine.

Afterward, Bob Stevens said to him, "Willie, when you caught that ball, I cried."

"Ah, come on, Bob," Willie said, grinning. "You didn't think I was going to drop it, did you?"

The Giants headed for the airport in Los Angeles, to return to San Francisco, where tomorrow they would open the World Series against the Yankees. (Shades of '51 all over again!)

When they reached San Francisco, the pilot came on the intercom to tell them they couldn't land.

Why? Because 75,000 San Franciscans had taken over the airport. They had barged onto the runways, broken through police lines, caused six regular flights to be diverted to the Oakland airport.

Finally the Giant plane got down. It pulled up at the United Air Lines maintenance hangar, a full mile from the terminal, but the crowd sensed the diversion, and came rushing full-tilt.

It was a mob—delirious, uncontrollable, singing, chanting.

The Giants were herded onto a bus.

The mob surrounded the bus.

Thousands upon thousands of them, they chanted and yelled.

"We want Willie! We want Willie!"

CHAPTER THIRTY

THE FIERCE LOVE

The 1962 World Series was, let's face it, an anti-climax. The Giants, probably the better team, didn't win. They lost it in seven. Mays doubled with two out in the last of the ninth of the final game, to put Matty Alou on third as the tying run and himself on second as the winning run. But Willie McCovey lined out. It was exciting, and everybody remembered afterward the old saying that baseball is a game of inches, but the Yanks won that game 1–0, and the Series 4 games to 3.

By common consent, the Giants won most of the glory and more gold than they'd had any right to expect. The exhaustion and strange "losing" nature of the final weeks of the pennant race, plus day upon day of rain which made

The bat swung by Number 24 drove in many of the runs that enabled the 1962 San Francisco Giants to lift the pennant right out of the hands of the foundering Los Angeles Dodgers.

the '62 Series the most prolonged in half a century, detracted from the ordinary glamour and tension of the Fall Classic, even though it went seven games and down to the last hitter.

After the Series, Mays spent a week barnstorming, to fulfill previous commitments. Then he came home, to learn that in 1963 he would be the first player in the history of the National League to earn a salary of $100,000.

He came home, too, to enter Mt. Zion Hospital in San Francisco for a thorough physical checkup.

The doctors found nothing wrong.

He came home, too, to buy a house, with the announcement that he was bringing his father—the legendary Kitty-Kat—from Birmingham to live with him in San Francisco, in the new house.

Throughout this story, as you know, we have been trying to pinpoint what it was that stamped Mays so far above all others—the spark, the inspiration, the quicksilver.

Perhaps the musical genius Leonard Bernstein said it best.

"Why is it?" he asked a television audience one time. "Why is it that one artist commands a fee ten times the amount any other artist can ask?"

And then he gave the answer.

"It is," he said, "because some people have a demon inside them—a fierce love for what they do."

And that, perhaps, more than anything else, tells the story of Willie Mays.

The fierce love. . .

Yet, to Willie, the most important thing, when he came

home to San Francisco following the 1962 season, was that one word itself:

Home.

He had found a home in the Giants' new city, just as he had in their old city—at long last.

From one coast to the other, the people knew.

What did they know?

That there was, and would be, only one Willie Mays.

THE WILLIE MAYS RECORD

Year	Club	League	G	AB	R	H	2b	3b	HR	RBI	B.Av.
1951	New York	National	121	464	59	127	22	5	20	68	.274
1952	In United States Army										
1953	In United States Army										
1954	New York	National	151	565	119	195	33	13	41	110	.345
1955	New York	National	152	580	123	185	18	13	51	127	.319
1956	New York	National	152	578	101	171	27	8	36	84	.296
1957	New York	National	152	585	112	195	26	20	35	97	.333
1958	San Fran.	National	152	600	121	208	33	11	29	96	.347
1959	San Fran.	National	151	575	125	180	43	5	34	104	.313
1960	San Fran.	National	153	595	107	190	29	12	29	103	.319
1961	San Fran.	National	154	572	129	176	32	3	40	123	.308
1962	San Fran.	National	162	621	130	189	36	5	49	141	.304
		Totals	1534	5862	1143	1846	301	99	368	1076	.315

WORLD SERIES RECORD

Year	Club	League	G	AB	R	H	2b	3b	HR	RBI	B.Av.
1951	New York	National	6	22	1	4	0	0	0	1	.182
1954	New York	National	4	14	4	4	1	0	0	3	.286
1962	San Fran.	National	7	28	3	7	2	0	0	1	.250
		Totals	17	64	8	15	3	0	0	5	.234

Sports Shelf Biographies You Will Enjoy

Henry Aaron: Quiet Superstar
by Al Hirshberg

Tom Seaver of the Mets
by George Sullivan

Ernie Banks: Mr. Cub
by Bill Libby

Tony Conigliaro: Up From Despair
by Robert Rubin

Babe Ruth: His Story in Baseball
by Lee Allen

Dizzy Dean
by Lee Allen

Ken Boyer
by David Lipman

Lou Gehrig: A Quiet Hero
by Frank Graham

Mickey Mantle: Mr. Yankee
by Al Silverman

My Ups and Downs in Baseball
by Orlando Cepeda with Charles Einstein

Roberto Clemente: Batting King
by Arnold Hano

Roy Campanella: A Man of Courage
by Gene Schoor

Sandy Koufax: Strikeout King
by Arnold Hano

Stan Musial: Baseball's Durable "Man"
by Ray Robinson

Ted Williams
by Ray Robinson

Willie Mays: Coast to Coast Giant
by Charles Einstein

THE AUTHOR

Author of several novels, hundreds of articles in major magazines, editor of the *Fireside Book of Baseball,* and author of television and movie scripts, Charles Einstein is a devoted Giant fan. He resided in the New York area to write about the team when they were based in New York City; he moved to a desert mountain home in Scottsdale, Arizona, not far from the Giant training grounds in Phoenix; and he now lives in Mill Valley, California, near San Francisco, with his wife and four children. He is also the author of *Born to Play Ball* by Willie Mays with Charles Einstein and *A Flag for San Francisco.*